YOUR MULTI-DIMENSIONAL WORKBOOK

Exercises For Energetic Awakening

Elaine Seiler

Your Multi-Dimensional Workbook, *Exercises for Energetic Awakening*
by Elaine Seiler
Copyright © 2011.

All rights reserved. No part of this book may be reproduced,
or utilised in any form or by any means, electronic or mechanical,
without permission in writing from the publisher or author.

Proofreader/Designer: Jennifer McMahon
Cover Design: Sara Dismukes

First Published by Transformation Energetics
204 Spring St
Marion, MA.02738
www.multi-dimensionalyou.com

In Association with Dog Ear Publishing
4010 W. 86th Street, Suite H
Indianapolis, IN 46268
www.dogearpublishing.net

ISBN: 978-145750-630-7

This book is printed on acid-free paper.

Printed in the United States of America

Dedication

TO PIONEERS of every sort, in every realm:

May they be supported by guides in body and out...to ease their way!
May they be blessed with self-confidence and courage as they forge ahead,
creating new physical and energetic pathways for those who follow!

Acknowledgements

MANY THANKS GO TO ALL WHO ASSISTED AND SUPPORTED ME during the process of creating this workbook, especially the guides whose training enabled me to offer these exercises and guidelines to others.

Special thanks to Jan Piraino, friend, transpersonal analyst, and channel par excellence. Without her metaphysical skills, this book would not exist.

To Jennifer McMahon whose diligence and patience resulted in the form of the workbook you see before you today.

To Sara Dismukes for the execution of the cover design. To Cyrene Houdini, whose skill facilitated the promotional videos for this project.

To Zsa Zsa Bacaling for her invaluable assistance in expanding my connections in the social media.

To Khepe-Ra Maat-Het-Heru, for her invaluable feedback and enthusiastic embrace of my work.

And finally, great appreciation to all those who asked me probing questions that clarified my thinking as I prepared this workbook. Thank you all.

CONTENTS

Introduction 1

Chapter 1   Multi-Dimensional Awakening 3

Chapter 2   Your Inner Energy Worker 7

Chapter 3   Language Of Energy 9

Chapter 4   Guides, Guidance And Energetics 13

Chapter 5   Journey Before Energetics 19

Chapter 6   Body As Instrument 29

Chapter 7   Visible Tools Of An Invisible Trade 55

Chapter 8   A Multi-Dimensional Conversation 65

Chapter 9   By-Products Of Energy Work 71

Chapter 10   Blended State 75

Chapter 11   Midwife To The Stars 83

Chapter 12   Multi-Dimensional Partnering 87

Chapter 13   Dream Interpretation: A Multi-Dimensional Perspective 91

Chapter 14   Creating A Multi-Dimensional Business 95

Chapter 15   Manifestation In A Multi-Dimensional World 97

Chapter 16   Fourth-Dimensional State 111

Chapter 17   Who Is In Charge? 115

Chapter 18   The End: The Beginning 119

Glossary of Definitions   An Energetic Perspective 121

Introduction

YOUR PATH TO MULTI-DIMENSIONALITY MAY BE GRADUAL or rapid, bumpy, or smooth, exhilarating and challenging. However it unfolds, it will be your unique process.

I have created this manual or workbook to ease your journey over those rough places, to hopefully enable your path to be smoother, quicker and gentler.

This workbook will follow a set format. I will introduce the theme or focus of a given chapter, give some examples and then offer a series of exercises to enable you to learn or improve your skills. Spaces have been provided after each exercise for you to record your answers or what you have learned. Don't forget to include your ah-ha moments.

I have found that when I understand a process, I can navigate it more easily and gracefully. When I don't understand, I flounder and make all kinds of incorrect assumptions about what I don't know, what I am doing wrong, what I could do better. By sharing my journey and offering you a series of exercises, I hope to make your path more comprehensible and therefore easier and more pleasurable to navigate. Please remember that you are learning new skills or awakening old dormant ones. Such learning requires time and practice. Do not expect mastery overnight or after one attempt at any given exercise. Practice. Give yourself a few days rest and practice again. Be gentle with yourself and honor yourself for doing the best you can with each attempt.

Make this an adventure, rather than a struggle. The evolutionary path on which you find yourself is unfolding with or without your understanding, with or without your participation. You might as well be as conscious as you can and enjoy as much of it as you can. Grab your hat, your magic carpet, your crystal wand or whatever you feel will assist the process and have fun as you walk forward to becoming MULTI-DIMENSIONAL YOU.

CHAPTER 1

Multi-Dimensional Awakening

"Awakening to the unseen world has changed and enriched my life. Where confusion, anxiety, depression, and hopelessness abound around me, my dimensional opening has given me an increased feeling of wellbeing, a stronger sense of security and a new level of faith and confidence. Although all may not look right in the world, at a deep level I trust it is right."*

ENERGIES ARE SWIRLING AROUND US ALL THE TIME, every moment. Often they are unbalanced. Energy workers consciously and unconsciously clear, balance and harmonize the energies in a given field. I do this work all the time; I consider it my profession. Most people, however, do it some of the time, while they proceed to live their lives and do all sorts of other jobs.

You can awaken the *energy worker* in you; you can become an energy worker. It may take a bit of time and effort, but I believe that each person has the innate ability just by being human to work with the energies of the Universe for the betterment of humankind and the planet.

Before we go further, let me define what I mean by an *energy worker*. Such a person uses his or her body to clear, balance and harmonize the unseen energies of the Universe. Those energies come from beyond the third dimension and use the physical body as the instrument through which to facilitate the greatest good for the greatest number of beings and the planet.

When the energies around us are calm and balanced, goals can be achieved; when the energies are chaotic, intentions are thwarted. Massage therapists, Reiki masters, Shiatsu practitioners, acupuncturists, hands-on healers as well as many other practitioners of the healing arts may consider themselves energy workers and may, in fact, do energy work, as I define it.

•The italicized quotations at the beginning of each chapter throughout this Workbook are from the companion book, Multi-Dimensional YOU, *Exploring Energetic Evolution*, written by Elaine Seiler.

The energy work, of which I speak in the book, "Multi-Dimensional YOU, *Exploring Energetic Evolution*" and in this workbook, does not require a particular set of physical skills or movements, or any sort of tangible tools or actions, of anything specific in physicality. The work of the energy worker is strictly vibrational. It exists in the invisible, intangible realms beyond the third dimension.

It is my hope that this handbook will increase your understanding of the unseen realms and facilitate your ability to consciously as well as actively participate with the intangible vibrations.

In this chapter, we will start the process of awakening your inner energy worker. We will begin by defining a field and then do some exercises to practice recognizing different fields.

The Field

A 'field' is the time/ space on which you are focused. A field might be defined as the room in which you sit, the neighbourhood in which you walk, the county or continent on which you live. And it is complicated by the fact that it is not a physical space, it is an invisible time/space location that stretches horizontally and vertically to include the energy of the people in it, the unseen vibrations of what is occurring geographically, politically, economically, socially, culturally, geologically and astronomically. At any one moment, there may be multiple frequencies crossing and criss-crossing the field. We are affected by all of them yet we have been unaware of them. You are about to take off your 'dimensional blinders' and become aware.

EXERCISE
Sensing The Field

Stop and pay attention to the place where you are right at this moment. How does it feel? Does it seem calm or chaotic? Is it comfortable or uncomfortable? It could be that you are in a time/space where there is lots of activity like a very busy Starbucks coffee shop or you may be home alone in your kitchen, either space may be calm or chaotic; the energy doesn't depend on the activity present. Is there a part of you wishing to move, to find another location before reading any further? Can you 'see', 'hear', 'feel', 'touch' any of the reasons why the room or locale seems the way it does?

Now, go beyond your five senses, beyond the *rational* reasons why the room seems calm or chaotic. Tune in to the vibrations just below the surface that have nothing to do with what you know or see about the space. Feel or intuit what is going on in that field. Trust that your first impression is correct, even though you have no proof to support what you believe that you sense. Walk around the space, touch some items, talk to a few people and then stop and *feel* the energies again.

Now move into another room, space or field. If you are unable to shift locations at this time, just shift your focus from inside to outside or vice versa, or from nearby to far away. Does it feel the same? Has anything changed? Are you feeling more or less comfortable? Did you sense any change since your arrival or since your movement or shift in focus?

Please record your answers to questions posed above. Use the blank pages at the end of this chapter or start a journal of your own; whatever works best for you. These notations are an important record of your awakening.

If you felt no change or were unable to sense anything, don't be concerned. Relax and accept that this is where you are at this moment and applaud and love yourself for being willing to *try*. That is what counts.

NOTES

NOTES

CHAPTER 2

Your Inner Energy Worker

"My primary tool is energy—the unseen vibrations of life, both the energies of the three-dimensional world and the energies that come from the other dimensions beyond physicality; the core goal of my work is transformation."

I BELIEVE THAT EVERY INDIVIDUAL HAS AN INNER *energy worker*, however each worker may do that work differently. Each of us has unique skills and abilities. In this section, you will begin to identify your unique capabilities. Questions have been provided to focus your thoughts on how you work energetically. Spaces have been left after each question for your answers.

EXERCISE

- Are you naturally a catalyst for change?

- Are you the one who always cleans up the mess? Perhaps you do it socially and physically. What about *energetically?*

- Do you function as the connective link between people? Are you a super networker? Do you intuitively know the appropriate person to introduce your new acquaintance to?

- Do you ever feel that what you are experiencing is not your own—not your own emotions, stress or fear? Have you ever thought about this, but didn't understand it and therefore just ignored it?

- Have you ever had the sense that it was your presence, rather than what you said or did that mattered? Did you bury that thought because you couldn't validate it?

- Ask yourself, "Is it possible that I have been working with energy all my life, but have never considered that idea before?"

KEEP THESE QUESTIONS IN YOUR MIND as you become more and more awakened to the dimensional reality around you. Trust that you are more than what you say and more than what you do. Your energetic presence may be your essential gift!

NOTES

CHAPTER 3

Language of Energy

*"Energy doesn't communicate in English, French, Chinese or Swahili,
but it does speak clearly."*

ENERGY DOESN'T COMMUNICATE IN ANY OF THE LANGUAGES we know. It speaks through the rains, floods, cyclones and earthquakes of nature, through the aches and pains of our bodies, through the seeming miracles of synchronicity and coincidence, through the metaphors present in color, shape and symbol and through the messages of our dreams and what we read and see and intuit from our everyday lives.

In this chapter we will explore the language of energy. The exercises provided will give you the opportunity to practice interpreting the energies you have encountered in the past and those you encounter every day as you go about your life.

EXERCISE

As you read the following questions, please consider the metaphors present in everything around you. Look at your emotional reactions as metaphors for the energy in the field. Pay attention to the irregularities in the field that might indicate that energy is speaking its message. Examine and attempt to interpret the metaphors suggested to you by each of the following questions. Note your observations after each question in the space provided.

- Are there flow and balance or restriction and constriction in the environment around you? What might nature be saying in the form of a metaphor?

- Examine your emotional state. What does it indicate about your energetic condition or the state of the field around you?

- Examine the people, places, things and situations in your life. Is there a satisfying and well-balanced inter-connectedness between them? Are there gaps or rifts that indicate breaks in the energetic flow?

- Are there any recurring themes in your life that reflect your current energetic state? Is water a predominant theme? Are there water leaks, blockages, and floods or pump breakdowns? What might these tell you about what is going on in your life or in your world? Is there too much e-motion or energy or not enough? Remember this may not be personal at all, but a reflection of what is happening in the field around you.

- Does your back ache or are your arms weary from carrying too many burdens?

- Are your sinus's weeping from the grief in the field?

- Do you hear *poorly* because you do not wish to hear the messages coming from the field around you or that the frequencies around you are so discordant as to be impossible to tolerate?

- Can you *see* only with difficulty because what you see or sense energetically is too painful to see physically?

- Are you unable to smell because something in your field is so rotten as to be unbearable?

- Are your fingers numb from energetically holding onto something too long or too tightly?

NOTES

NOTES

CHAPTER 4

Guides, Guidance and Energetics

"Guidance is more than inspiration or spiritual wisdom; it is insight that comes from the other dimensions beyond this physical realm. The Universe will use any vehicle and any medium to communicate with us. Our job is to be alert and to listen."

WHAT ABOUT INSPIRATION, INTUITON, PSYCHIC INPUT OR GUIDANCE? In this chapter we will explore these concepts. Hopefully, the information and exercises that follow will answer any questions that have come up about these ideas.

The key to understanding the answer to any questions about guidance is having a clear grasp of what is three-dimensional and what is *other*-dimensional. It matters not at all what a message is called, inspiration or intuition, psychic ability or guidance. What does matter is the source of the information.

If it is sourced beyond the veil, beyond the physical world, from the realms that are only energy, then I call that information *guidance*. It is not a reworking of something that has been on the planet before. It is not just new to you; it is different, unique, never been on the earth before. It comes from beyond the veil. I refer to that idea as *guidance*.

In the third dimension or physical realm, we can be inspired with an idea that we have never had before, but that idea might have existed somewhere in the physical world (though perhaps not in your field until that moment). I call that idea *inspiration* as it is sourced in the third dimension.

Guidance or intuition?

How does one tell the difference between intuition and guidance? How does one identify the source of one's information? Ah, that is the big question. It seems difficult, but you are about to discover that it is really quite clear and easy to determine.

If the information you receive is felt physically, it is sourced in the physical and is three-dimensional inspiration. If, on the other hand, the information is sensed outside of the body, it is energetic and coming from beyond the veil.

Guidance speaks in many different ways—through a disembodied voice in one's head, through the words of a book or newspaper, through an image that one passes on the street, through dreams, through the environment around us or via the reactions in our bodies that reflect the message of the environment around us.

Let's look at some examples. Try to distinguish which are physical inspiration or intuition and which are energetic and considered guidance. Please circle either *Guidance* or *Intuition* where indicated. At the end of the following list of examples, you will find the answers to the source of that specific inspiration.

EXERCISE

1. You are driving through your home town. You always take a particular route and suddenly you feel a strong need to turn left, instead of right, thereby avoiding an accident blocking the next intersection.

    Guidance / Intuition

2. You are thinking about a friend, thinking you should give her a call, when the phone rings and it is your friend.

    Guidance / Intuition

3. I was meditating when my ill grandson died. I was actually conversing with him in my head. I suggested that if he was going to live, that he wake from his coma and come fully into his body or he should let go of the body and fully depart this life. I noted the time that I stopped meditating. When I checked with the nurse in the intensive care unit, he had died at exactly the minute I stopped meditating.

    Guidance / Intuition

4. Twenty years ago, I had no idea what energetics was or what was the role of an energy worker. Over the years I have received a great deal of information psychically that has formed the basis for the book, "Multi-Dimensional YOU", and this companion workbook.

    Guidance / Intuition

5. The dishwasher in my house in Australia overflowed. The pipe under the bathtub in my apartment in New York City disintegrated and leaked into my neighbor's apartment. The pump on my well broke down. I understood that the energies all around me were over-amped, too strong, too fast, and too intense for the systems that had once worked. They were not only physically old; their vibrations were energetically too slow to handle the more rapid vibrations of the energies (waters) of today. All the systems needed to be upgraded.

    Guidance / Intuition

6. I was at a large festival of dark skinned Gypsies and light skinned European Catholics, both of whom were celebrating the special Feast of Les Trios Maries de la Mer (the Three Marys of the Sea) in southern France. The Catholics were praying to and cleansing the statue of Mother Mary. The Gypsies were celebrating with a statue of their patron saint, a black child, named Sarah. It was a well-attended and racially integrated festival. I very strongly felt the presence of a dear, dear Afro-American friend who was in a hospital in the US, dying from cancer. She walked with me during the festival. At the end of the day, I called to check on my friend's health. Her caregiver reported she was in and out of her body and was seemingly speaking nonsense. I asked what sort of nonsense. I was told that my friend was "thrilled because she was present at a gathering of many hundreds of people in which the blacks and the whites had gotten together". My friend died shortly after the event.

    Guidance / Intuition

7. While white water rafting on the Colorado River, I felt an excruciating pain in my gut when told we were going to navigate the most dangerous channel between the rocks. I *knew* it was not safe for me to go down the river with *that* boatman in *that* boat at *that* time. With some difficulty, I negotiated my way into one of the other boats. We managed to cross the rapids safely, but one of the boats did overturn and the occupants narrowly escaped the perils of the churning white water.

    Guidance / Intuition

Answers

1. *Inspired to change directions (other-dimensional **guidance**)*
2. *Knowing who is on the telephone (three-dimensional inspiration or **intuition**)*
3. *Ending my meditation at the exact time of my grandson's death (other-dimensional **guidance**)*
4. *Receiving the information for this book (other-dimensional **guidance**)*
5. *Recognizing the meaning of the of four concurrent water leaks (other- dimensional **guidance**)*
6. *Sensing my dying friend's presence with me in France (other-dimensional **guidance***
7. *Pre-cognitively knowing the dangers of forthcoming white water rafting experience (three-dimensional inspiration or **intuition**)*

THERE ARE MANY BOOKS THAT CAN ASSIST YOU IN OPENING your intuitive, psychic or telepathic abilities. I will not delve into that area for it is well covered elsewhere. I do, however, want to talk a bit about guidance.

I believe all souls have guides, angels, or disembodied beings that are present throughout their lives, guiding, nudging, pushing or shoving us out of harm's way and into greater and greater awareness. Our job is to open, to agree to receive. A guide cannot offer assistance if we are not open to it. That is the Law of the Universe.

Therefore, whether you have been aware of your guidance for years, or if you have never felt its presence, make or renew your commitment to sense and accept the guidance when it sits before you. It may be as gentle as butterfly wings or as loud as a booming voice. It is your choice to ask for it and to be willing to receive it.

Is it necessary for you to be aware of your guidance for you to do 'energy work' or for you to evolve? Not at all! As a matter of fact, I have a friend who squirms at the mere thought of input coming from outside her beingness and yet she is one of the most intuitive, psychically, spiritually and energetically aware people I know. It doesn't seem to matter what she calls her *knowing*. It does matter that she is *aware* of her knowing and that she listens to it.

NOTES

NOTES

CHAPTER 5

Journey before Energetics

"I was a being in disguise—ostensibly studying the American culture of the direct, outspoken, forthright and blatant, while actually immersing myself in the subtle, asymmetrical, indirect and soft-spoken world of the Orient. Even then (1962), I was seeking ways to bridge different worlds."

WHAT PATH DID YOU WALK TO GET WHERE you are today and what were some of the energetic stimuli that led you here?

Each of us has had a lifetime of experiences that seem random and without direction as they are occurring. They zig and zag and then miraculously they take us exactly where we need to go. In the 1970s when I was caring for four young babies under the age of seven, I never thought I would get away from diapers and baby formula. When I was teaching English in Japan I never imagined that my experience there would be a training ground for energetic awareness forty years later. It is only with hindsight that I understand how each experience offered me a myriad of opportunities to learn what I needed to move me forward on my life's path and prepare me for the next step in my evolution.

The next section of this workbook focuses on a review of your life. I am inviting you to do as I have done in Chapter 4 in my book, "Multi-Dimensional YOU, *Exploring Energetic Evolution*"... to consider your life from an energetic perspective.

PLEASE REVIEW THE VARIOUS SECTORS of your life—early childhood, teenage years, college or university, first jobs, marriage, children, professional training—or the significant life-changing events. There are pages allocated at the end of this chapter, to start your **Life Review**.

The following questions are offered to stimulate your thoughts.

- What did you do? Use action words.
- How did you do it? Use descriptive words.

- Why is this event important to you? Your values are revealed here. Please consider why you are writing about this particular experience now, rather than why you did it years ago. Why is it noteworthy to you, not to your parents, your partner or great Aunt Tilly?

IN THIS PART OF THE EXERCISE you will be writing a three-dimensional, physical description of what occurred. Take as much time as you need to do this life review. This is not something that can be done in ten minutes. Spend some time. Take a break and come back to the exercise. Give it the time and focus that it deserves. No matter how insignificant you judge a part of your life to be, it is valuable and will shed light on who you have become and what sort of energy work you intuitively are able to do.

Once you have completed the **physical description** of the events, please go back and write an **energetic description** of each event. Use the words you wrote to give you clues to the energetic perspective. Watch for words that indicate the metaphors present in your story.

"I couldn't breathe."

"I had difficulty digesting the food/experience."

"I felt like I was carrying the weight of the world on my shoulders."

"I heard so much more than he was saying."

"I felt trapped in a prison."

"The feeling in the room was unbelievably high, we were ecstatic."

NOTES

NOTES

TO WRITE THIS ENERGETIC INTERPRETATION, stand, as if on a giant pedestal, from which you are able to see with different, far-seeing eyes and view your life's unfolding from that meta-perspective. Remember, you are no longer focused on what happened physically or what you felt emotionally, psychologically or spiritually. You are to uncover an awareness of the energies that you were working with at that time and you are extracting insights about those energies as they played out through your life's experience.

Ask yourself, did you...

- sense the energies?
- clear the energies?
- balance the energies?
- calm and quiet the energies?
- lift and vitalize the energies?
- harmonize the energies?
- connect disparate energies?
- separate overly entangled energies?
- educate others about the energies?
- deliver energetic messages?

LET'S LOOK AT A FEW MORE EXAMPLES before you get started.

Example 1

In 1962 I spent six months in Japan teaching English and living with a Japanese family. When I returned to the US to complete my college degree, I wrote a paper on the school as a microcosm of the Japanese society.

Physical perspective

1. What did I do?

   I taught English in a foreign country. I lived with a foreign family. I probed both the world of the junior high school and the larger society for their values and I compared them.

2. How did I do it?

   Diligently. Carefully. Thoroughly.

3. Why is my experience in Japan important to me?

   I learned how to relate to those who were different. I learned how to effectively communicate, to observe, to teach and to bridge cultural differences. I learned that the small often reflects the large.

Energetic perspective

I was a stranger in a strange land. I observed the culture and mimicked it. Some patterns were physical and blatant; other were invisible and I had to pay attention to the subtle, sensed rather than seen clues. I learned who I was away from my biological family and away from my own culture and country.

At that time, I had no awareness of energies or how I used them. I only knew I was able to adapt and to adapt well, to share, and to teach. In retrospect, I now understand that I was learning to relate to different energy fields, to pick up subtle unseen clues about the people and the environment and to create bridges between the different worlds.

Example 2

You are a shop owner. You created the business from the ground up. You designed your shop and determined what to sell. And, you are very successful, even when the economy is down. People love to come into your shop; they come by to chat, even when they don't intend to buy something.

When you look at your experience in your business, you realize that the energy you create in your shop is as, if not more important, than the merchandise you have to sell. You create the field. You create a bridge between yourself and the customer. You smooth and soothe the energies so that those who visit feel calm and comfortable and want to return. They return and they buy. Yes, you are good at choosing your merchandise, but the energy you unconsciously and inadvertently create is the key to your success.

Example 3

Or you are a writer. You write about all sorts of topics, literally anything that catches your attention—the latest news, the crisis in a foreign government, the long line of people in the supermarket. When you write you share the meta-perspective. You share your observations about the energies present not just what you see or hear.

You never realized that before, but when you probe your writing history, you realize your writing is different than other commentators. You start with what occurred, but you never leave it there. You always share something about the unseen realms that most people pay little or no attention to. It has contributed to your success, but until now, you never labeled it *energetic*.

YOU ARE NOW READY AND, I HOPE, EAGER TO START your life review. Write as much or as little as you desire—phrases or pages—the length of your description is not important. What is critical is that you probe your history for clues as to how you, as an individual, function in the world of energy.

As you probe your past with this energetic lens, please note how these skills play out in your life today. Are you discovering you do, indeed, have an inner energy worker, that you are a multi-dimensional being and that life is richer and more fascinating then you ever imagined? Begin today to honor yourself for the unseen energy work that you do.

If you get stuck, leave the exercise temporarily. Continue on through the workbook and then come back to this exercise as you become more familiar with the multi-dimensional world.

START YOUR LIFE REVIEW HERE

LIFE REVIEW

LIFE REVIEW

LIFE REVIEW

CHAPTER 6

Body As Instrument

"In my very first aware job as an energy worker, I jokingly referred to myself as a cosmic vacuum cleaner, cleaning and clearing the spaces and people around me. This continues to be an apt description of what I do. The energies playing through me alter and balance the space around me. Personality Elaine does nothing to consciously affect the change. Energetic Elaine is present so that the energy of the other dimensions can move through me to shift the energies that are present."

YOUR BODY IS AN AMAZING INSTRUMENT OF ENERGETIC PROCESSING. It is capable of doing a myriad of jobs of which you may be totally unaware.

Those abilities not only run your physical structure and inner workings as a biological organism, but also can facilitate your interaction with the seen and unseen environment to create harmony and balance around you. This interaction is energetic and invisible. To make these processes clear and easier to understand, I have given them physical descriptors.

In this section we will explore your abilities and do some exercises to awaken or improve your skills in identifying them. Remember, each of us is unique and has distinct abilities, given to us because they are exactly what we need in our lives. You may have some, none, or all of the following capacities. Whatever your skills, please honor them and do not compare your abilities to others or denigrate what you do, because others around you do something else. I spent many years feeling inadequate because my skills seemed lacking when compared to those around me. That was not true, my abilities were just different.

The following are thirteen of the principle jobs or processes I have uncovered that are done by those working with energy. There may be others. Feel free to add to this list. After each job label, I give a brief description and an example from my own life. Become familiar with each of these. At the end of the chapter, you will find a series of exercises that are designed to awaken your energetic awareness and assist you to recognize your unique blend of energetic skills.

Types of Energy Work

1. *Cosmic Vacuum Cleaner*

The *cosmic vacuum cleaner* clears and cleans the energetic space and the people in his or her field. Most often, this is done unconsciously.

I am very sensitive to motor vibrations. I often have to check out several hotel rooms to ensure that I am away from air conditioner compressors or ice machines. Over the years I have learned that my movement in and out of four or five hotel rooms in a given hotel, is way more than just a search for a comfortable room.

It is an opportunity for my body to clear and clean the energies in that hotel in that city in that country at that particular time. This process is often irksome emotionally and physically, but valuable from the energetic perspective.

2. *Anchor*

An energetic *anchor* grounds the energy of whomever and whatever is present in a given field. I am most aware of doing this job with my children or friends when they are excited, stressed and spinning with emotion. As we progress through the conversation or meeting, they will often tell me that they feel better—calmer or more balanced than before they called or visited me.

This process is also evident in a room or field in which the energies are highly charged and escalating. I have been intuitively guided to places where the resistors to a political or economic situation were marching in protest. I was present on the sidelines and told that my presence helped to ground the energies present.

3. *Bellows/ Damper*

As a *bellows* or *damper*, the person working with energy either lifts and increases the energies when they are low and sluggish or lowers and decreases the energies when they are too fiery and volatile.

I was most aware of playing this role as I travelled in India and South East Asia. I was compelled to wear bright colours, cobalt blue, emerald green, fuchsia, bright orange, or hot pink all through my trip. I was aware I was activating the energies around me. A higher, faster vibration was needed to maximize whatever was going on in India at that time.

As soon as I returned to America and Australia, those fast vibrations were no longer needed. I could no longer wear those fiery colors. They felt wrong and grating to my system. For a very long time after that trip I wore pale blues and greens, soothing, cooling, calming tones that 'dampened' and cooled the frequencies around me that were now too fiery and explosive.

4. Tuning Fork

A person acting as an energetic *tuning fork* harmonizes the vibrations in the field so they are aligned and resonant. This is most easily evidenced wherever diverse groups of people are gathered—in restaurants, concert halls, bus terminals and airports, for example. The energies pass through the 'tuning fork', resonate to the note or frequency of the one acting as the tuning fork and radiate out into the space to harmonize the disparate frequencies present.

I have unconsciously done this 'job' in many locations all over the globe. It's as if the energy worker is singing a note and holding it long enough for everyone else in the room to sing along, but there is no song and there are no audible notes. The process is energetic and unseen.

5. Messenger, Seed Sower, Janie Appleseed

Energetic *Janie Appleseeds* knowingly and unknowingly carry vibrations from one field to another all the time, seeding new ideas as they go.

In 2001 under the aegis of a new business entity, ReGenesis Enterprises, I established an organic farm or a laboratory for innovative agricultural concepts in New South Wales, Australia. We initiated several new ideas, growing on hay bales, farming without chemicals, commencing a bio-recycling project and establishing a soil composting company that used the organic waste from the bio-recycling project. Not only were these ideas introduced to the community, but also they were literally seeded into the land, to take root and hopefully flourish in the future.

6. Lightning Rod

Acting as a *lightning rod*, some people act as attractors of frequencies. I am aware, for example, that my clothes and jewelry often draw the attention of those around me. By magnetizing individuals to me, positively or negatively, an energetic pathway is created between us that enable my energies to reach out and blend with, harmonize or shift the energies of others. It is as if a bolt of lightning lights up the sky around me, attracting all in the field to that one spot or person.

7. Resonator

Energy workers are *resonators*, vibrating whatever frequencies are required into the field. The worker then pulls the frequencies back into and through his or her body like a filter system and then sends them back into the field again and again until most or all of the energies present are harmonized and synchronized.

I have been part of several very discordant groups. There were no obvious values, interests or cultural conflicts to be processed; there were no recognizable areas of disharmony. Yet, there was discordance. This problem and its solution rested in the energetic realm.

8. *Transducer*

Transduction of physical substances is present when the warmth of hot water becomes scalding heat, when cool dew becomes cold rain or icy rain becomes lethal balls of hail. I, and others, act as energetic *transducers* when we allow our bodies to be used as transforming devices for other dimensional energies. As the higher, faster energies of the other dimensions descend through the body's natural transduction system, the rapid energies are transduced into slower vibrations that are useable by the physical body here on earth.

9. *Field Holder*

As an energetic *field holder*, an energy worker maintains the balance of a varied mix of frequencies in a given space-time environment.

Have you ever been at a meeting during which you or someone else meditated during the session? Just by being present, that person silently wove the energies into a melodious tapestry that held the mood, emotions and energies of the participants in harmony and alignment so that the highest goals could be met.

Another way to understand a field holder is to imagine someone holding a handful of kite strings. These strings however, are virtual and are not connected by any physical objects; they are connected to the various energies present in the field. As the field holder pulls or releases the invisible strings, they literally hold the web of the space together and anchor it into the ground so that it is steady and secure and will not change or dissipate in the presence of stronger, bolder or slower frequencies.

10. **Grid Holders**

Grid holders use a wide range of frequencies to keep the energy structure around the planet balanced and stable. Some energy workers focus their efforts on keeping the poles of the planet in place, relatively speaking.

In March 2011, when Japan was rocked by earthquakes and tsunamis, the energy workers of the planet worked over-time to attempt to keep the poles in place and to avert even more devastation than what occurred.

11. *Reflector*

Energy workers also act as *reflectors*, taking into their bodies the frequencies coming from the grid, processing those vibrations through their physical instrument like a filtration system, expressing or reflecting those vibrations out into the world as a variety of concepts.

In 2011, as the world experienced the full range of unusual climatic, geological and political conditions, my body mimicked or reflected the floods, cyclones and revolutions. I experienced unusual emotional clarity, physical strength and determination as well as serious nasal congestion and an excess of body fluids, and as revolutions shook the Arab world, the stability of my own personal world was also coming apart.

12. *Perturbator*

Perturbators are energy workers who catalyse a disturbance in the field that has a rippling effect like a pebble thrown into a pond.

In 1995, I lived for one year in Jackson Hole, Wyoming. When I moved out of my home there, I was intuitively guided to give a friend all my Bach Flower remedies. In 2011, I received the following email note: "I'll never forget the day you arrived at my door with boxes of flower essences and your announcement: 'I'm supposed to give these to you.' I didn't get it at first, but gradually found that friends were coming to me with their various problems and would look favorably on trying the essences. Since I've gotten more adept at using a pendulum I have relied on that method to determine which essences are appropriate. I've enjoyed being able to help in that way, and thank you for encouraging me!" wrote my friend.

13. *Bridge (Between People)*

Energy workers create energetic *bridges between people*, facilitating communication and understanding often without words. When I attend any sort of meeting, seminar, or conference, I am aware that I am present for far more than to learn a new system or teach a new process. I am present to create energetic pathways between all those present. I don't *do* anything consciously. I merely allow the energies to move through me and do what they do, creating as many links as possible between those present. It is a little like creating 'friends' on Facebook or connections on LinkedIn; the only difference is that it is all done virtually, without a computer, with the energies that flow through our bodies naturally.

14. *Bridge (Between Dimensions)*

Finally, we come to the last of the jobs of the energy worker—being a *bridge between dimensions*.... Energy workers create energetic pathways between dimensions, assisting souls to leave their physical bodies and pass over to the other side of the veil.

I had a very strong experience of this when I suddenly felt as if I had developed a hunchback condition. I have never felt that way before or since. That day as I complained of my sudden, uncomfortable back condition, I read in the newspaper about the death of Mother Teresa. For those who do not know, Mother Teresa had a severe hunchback-like condition. I believe that I assisted her to pass over to the other side of the veil.

I have also had the experience of assisting disembodied souls to cross the veil and materialize into physicality without going through the normal gestation and birthing process. I cannot prove this to you, but I believe it is true. Perhaps in time, you too will have this experience and can assist me in substantiating it as fact.

Now that you have a clear idea of the jobs that your inner energy worker might do, theoretically, let us probe a little deeper and explore what jobs you have each personally done.

What are your unique gifts as an energy worker?
EXERCISE 1

Please return to the entries you made in the last chapter. Go back over them, section by section and in a contrasting colored pen, add the descriptors you have just learned for each of the jobs you did. If you are not sure, guess. If you don't believe, act as if you believe. This is merely an opportunity for you to begin to think in terms of the descriptive energetic phrases that I have found so very useful. If you come up with other descriptors, perfect. Accept and use them and trust that they are correct for you.

Write your notes for this section in the space left at the end of each exercise.

NOTES

EXERCISE 2

To facilitate the process of identifying the kind of energy work that you do, I have listed a series of questions below. Use these questions to trigger your memories of your energetic experiences. You have had them. They are just hidden away. With a little focus they will resurface. Please make notes on your energetic experiences in the space provided.

- Have you ever sat quietly with a friend or family member holding space for them to rest, recuperate, adjust to a new life situation or cross the veil?

    If you have done this, you were an energetic *field holder*.

- Were there times in your life, when you cleaned up after everyone, physically and emotionally? What about energetically?

    If you have cleaned up energetically, you were acting as a *cosmic vacuum cleaner*.

- Have you ever meandered around a meeting hall before a conference, feeling the space, imagining you could clear the energies with your mind and then all of sudden, you felt a subtle shift? The room felt different. Perhaps you were clearing the space and you didn't even know it.

    You were being an energetic *vacuum cleaner*.

- Can you remember a time when your friends or children were so excited on the goodness of life that you found yourself becoming very, very quiet, grounding 'calmness' in the space?

    Such behavior is acting as an energetic *anchor*.

- Did you ever act as an energetic messenger, an idea seed sower?

  In doing so, you were a *Janie Appleseed*.

- Have you acted as an attractor, drawing all the energies in a space to you? Or have you noticed an individual whose vibrations were so strong that all in the room noticed and watched him, even though he said nothing and did nothing unusual at all?

  Such an attractor was acting as an energetic *lightning rod*.

- What is it about your energy and your best friend or life partner that makes the two of you so resonant? How does that differ from someone in your book group who reads the same books as you, but may have very different energies?

  Such an alignment of energies indicates you were an energetic *resonator*.

- Have you experienced illness, aches, pains or strong emotions that you felt were not yours? In retrospect can you see that you might have been reflecting what was going on in the field at that time?

  Were you a *reflector*?

- Have you experienced or witnessed a dramatic shift in emotion from a very strong state to a more moderate one, due to the presence of an individual, with no words or process?

  Was an energetic *transducer* present?

- Has your presence amped-up the energies of a project or celebration? Did you act as an energetic *amplifier*?

- Have your energies calmed and harmonized the energies of a project or celebration?

  Were you an energetic *damper*?

- Have you ever acted as a bridge between diverse people or groups of people in ways that had nothing to do with the content of your communication or your actions and everything to do with your vibrations?

  Were you a *bridge between people*?

- Have you had any experience or can you fantasize having any experience about being a bridge to the beings in the other-dimensional realms?

  Have you ever been a *bridge between dimensions*?

NOTES

IF YOU ARE HAVING DIFFICULTY DOING THE REVIEW of your life history, then let the process go. Let's try the following exercises instead.

EXERCISE 3

Focus on a time and place of your choice. It could be your kitchen this morning, your dining room last evening or your place of business today. Think back on the people present, the furniture, the accessories, the temperature, the amount of light and décor in this space.

Now shift your focus beyond the physical people and things present to the unseen energies that swirl in and around the field. Allow your inner knowing to sense/feel what kind of vibrations were present. Were they calm and balanced, chaotic and jagged, soft and gentle or wild and frantic?

I am asking you to *read* the invisible energies, not recount the number of people present or the sounds they made.

- Did you feel comfortable?
- What influences were present?
- What, if anything, were you feeling?

You felt angry, but didn't know why. Or you felt extremely exhausted and drained, but there was no ostensible reason for this level of fatigue. Make an effort to distinguish between physical and energetic exhaustion.

- Did your energy level change during the time/space?
- When?
- Why?
- What signs did you note of your shift from a denser energy field to a lighter, more rapid one or vice versa?

Be aware that we often tell ourselves stories based on a physical experience about what we are sensing to explain the unseen, when, in fact, there is often no evidence for that particular story at all. I might, for example, tell myself that I am feeling isolated and alone because I have no partner. In fact, I may be feeling isolated and alone at that moment because three of the women present in my field have recently lost their husbands and were physically, emotionally and energetically bereft. I was feeling what they were feeling.

Or I might feel tired and blame it on a poor night's sleep, when energetically, it is actually because I am working very hard to balance the divergent energies in the group.

Every environment you enter is a field. Every field is large (a continent) or small (your dining room) depending on your focus. Every field is more or less balanced. Your job may be to clear and balance that space/time environment. It is as if you become an orchestra conductor, weaving the energies into a melodious symphony or a juggler balancing a dozen balls, not with your hands, but with your very beingness. As you move through the space, as you turn and twist, as you raise and lower your vibrations, you affect and balance the vibrations around you.

As a result, it is as if a melody is heard or a magnificent painting is created, through the balancing of the invisible threads. The challenging part is there is no visible manifestation. The result is felt, however, for at the energetic level it is as real as if there were substance present.

NOTES

EXERCISE 4

Stand in a room, any room or space will do. Imagine yourself as a musical instrument sending out notes into the space. Pull notes into and through your body over and over again, until all the notes floating in the space are balanced or aligned. Allow your own creative capacity to create the image for you. You may see a picture with all the contents neatly lined in a row. You may see a scale with the elements balanced from one side to the other. You may hear harmony of sounds. You may feel that there is balance and harmony, but not see or hear anything at all.

I cannot predict how you will experience the balance or lack of it in a given field, but I assure you, you will sense it. In the past you might have attributed it to the physical circumstances. In this exercise I am asking you to by-pass the physical interpretation and focus on the unseen realms.

Focus on what your intuition tells you. Focus on the messages of your body. Focus on the clues from nature. If you can't identify anything other than what your five senses are telling you, that is fine too. Just note what you do feel and go on.

NOTES

EXERCISE 5

Now, shift gears and go to another place or visit the same space at a different time. There might be other people present, or no one present.

- Note how you feel or what you notice.
- What are you sensing?
- Does it feel different than your first or earlier visit?
- Shift your focus to what contributed to the changes you feel. How did your presence affect the field?

NOTES

EXERCISE 6

Please try the above exercises a few times a week in different kinds of spaces or environments until you feel you have uncovered your energetic eyes and activated your energetic feelers. Please make notes on all your experiences.

NOTES

NOTES

Exploring One's Sensitivities

The following exercises are slightly different to the ones you have just completed. The prior exercises hopefully revealed your innate capabilities as an energy worker.

The next exercises will help you to understand your tolerance levels and your threshold for doing energy work without becoming drained or depleted.

EXERCISE 1

Focus on a specific experience, any experience of your choice. Review it in your mind's eye. Explore the energetic as well as the physical effects on you of the place, the people, the food and drinks you consumed, the content of the conversations, the social, economic, geo-political events happening in other parts of the world.

In the space for notes write a brief description of the experience on which you focused, describing it physically and then energetically.

Pay attention to your fatigue level. What aspects of the field drained your energy? Try to distinguish between physical and energetic exhaustion.

What are the unique signals your body gives you that you have had enough, that you have reached your limit of interaction?

NOTES

EXERCISE 2

Go into two different noisy restaurants or stores and two different quiet restaurants or stores. Compare your experience. Probe past the noise or quiet, to the energy or vibration beneath the audible range of sound or the actual number of people present.

You may find that one fully occupied restaurant is actually more balanced and comfortable for you than the almost empty restaurant. In the latter, there might be a mysterious energy which you cannot define or explain, but that is deeply jarring to your being; its vibrations are totally discordant and unbalanced.

Record what you learn about your sensitivities and your level of energetic tolerance.

NOTES

NOTES

Energetic Clearing

Energy never disappears; it never ceases. Therefore, we are all attempting to balance unseen vibrations all the time, 24/7. Fortunately, it is rare that all the possible energetic forces that could impact us, do affect us simultaneously. Most of the time, we are able to balance what we are exposed to.

Occasionally, however, the energies present in a given field are so many, so strong or so toxic (meaning out of alignment with our own frequencies) that we are unable to balance them. We become overloaded and need to clear ourselves before we can go on. This might mean that you look and feel ill with any number of symptoms. In actuality, your seeming illness is not caused by a bacteria or virus, but by the toxic overload of too many inputs causing an imbalance in your system.

When this occurs, you need a reprieve, while you clear your body as an instrument, refill your gas tank or energy quota and rebuilt your energetic core. This happens to all of us. Do not be distraught. Accept the situation and give your body and psyche the rest and nurturance they need.

There are many ways of clearing oneself. I find that withdrawing from the toxic environment to my own space where I can rebuild my energy field without having to interact with other energies is essential as the first step in rebalancing myself.

If possible, submerging myself in water in a bathtub at home (many times a day if necessary) or in salt water if one is lucky enough to be near a beach is one of the best solutions. If one can neither withdraw nor bathe, the following cleansing visualization is extremely helpful and can be done in one's mind, no matter what is going on, no matter where one might be.

EXERCISE

Clearing the overload

The following is a very powerful and effective visualization that you can do to facilitate energetic clearing.

> *IN YOUR MIND'S EYE, hold a mosquito screen and imagine gently passing it through your body. If you hit a place of resistance, turn the screen and pass it through your body in the other direction.*
>
> *If you are 'seeing' the screen move from the right side of your body to the left, move it instead from the left to the right. If you are passing it from the top to the bottom, shift and move it from the bottom to the top.*

Or move it in your mind, back and forth, back and forth, slowly over the same spot, loosening the energetic debris, until the screen moves all the way through.

When this process feels complete, visually scrape the yuck off the screen and drop it into a basket or container, held for you by beings in the subtle realms.

Ask them to remove the toxic waste, negative emotions, and environmental sludge and transmute it so that it can no longer affect you or others. Then trust that your body is clear and the toxic overload is removed.

OCCASIONALLY FULL CLEARANCE is not possible and you must try again at another time. Do not be disturbed if this occurs. Let it go and try again later. In time, the energies *will* shift.

Observe your reactions as the imaginary screen moves through your physical form. Did your physical body move as you moved your virtual screen?

Could you feel a relationship between the visualization, or what was occurring in the subtle realm, and your body in the physical world?

Even if you do not feel anything as you do this exercise, act as if you have actually cleared your physical form of the unwanted, unnecessary, debilitating toxic energies. In time, you will find that your sensitivities increase and you will actually experience the process.

If you hit a place of resistance, ask yourself what the blockage might be. Do not try to figure out the answer. Rather, allow the answer to pop into your mind. Allow your subconscious to speak to you. Allow your higher self to respond to the question from a deeper part of you. If an answer comes to consciousness, ask yourself what you must do to deal with that situation, that relationship, that challenge, whatever is blocking the clearing of your energy.

If you are unable to visualize the process I have described, just *think* it. Think yourself through the exercise in your mind. Continue with this thinking process whenever you intuitively feel it will be beneficial. Act as if you believe that you have actually cleared your physical form of the unwanted, unnecessary, debilitating toxic energies. One day you will be surprised to find that you are actually seeing and experiencing the passage of the screen and actually feeling the release of the toxicity in your body.

Motor vibrations are another form of toxicity. If you are affected by these vibrations and cannot avoid their presence, try to open yourself to all the vibrations present in the field, accepting, rather than resisting them. In so doing, you will *background* what is disturbing and *foreground* a smooth totality of vibrations. You cannot make those frequencies go away, but you can diminish their impact.

Please note your observations and share your perceptions about the energetics of your experiences with at least one other person to affirm your observations.

NOTES

EXERCISE

Sensing the truth: Is this mine or yours?

There is one more exercise I would like to offer you.

Sometimes our energies join the predominant vibrations in the field and we take on the emotions, confusion, anxiety, or fears that are present. They feel like ours, but in fact they are not.

Sometimes, we take on what is in the field so strongly that we reflect what is occurring around us in our bodies. If the field is congested, our nasal passages may become congested, or we may experience allergies, cramps or indigestion.

We have become over-whelmed, quite literally, and we experience the energies present around us as if they are our own. When this occurs we need to recognize what has occurred and then clear our energy field.

- Whenever you feel tired, drained or emotionally spent, ask yourself, "Is this mine?"

- Perhaps you felt fine when you arrived at the meeting and now you feel nauseous and dizzy. Ask yourself, "Is this mine?"

- At the end of a meeting or a day's work, when ou are not feeling yourself, please ask yourself, "Am I ill or is this a reaction to the vibrations present within the field?"

- If you feel dizzy, ask yourself, "Are the vibrations swirling around me in such a way as to literally be turning me in circles within which I cannot find my center?"

- You felt healthy and well when you left my home to go to the party, and now you feel as if you are coming down with a sore throat or flu. Ask yourself, "Am I truly physically sick or am I having a reaction to the energies present at the gathering?"

- You are feeling exhausted; you feel you can hardly speak, ask yourself, "Are the vibrations present so draining as to leave me speechless and weak? "

ASK YOURSELF QUESTIONS like these when you first notice physical symptoms of any sort. If necessary, remove yourself from the field in order to get a clearer sense of what is occurring.

Try not to think of yourself as sick, but rather as reflecting the energies present. If you focus on 'being ill' in any form, you will concretize the energies into a physical manifestation or 'illness'.

If you shift your thoughts to your 'well-being' and consider the energies with which you are dealing, you will be surprised at how often your symptoms will disappear when you are out of the field and away from the disturbing frequencies.

Note your awareness of your sensitivities. Raise any questions that come to you. Observe and record as much as you are able. Over time, you will become more and more skilled at noting what is truly physical and what is also truly energetic.

NOTES

NOTES

CHAPTER 7

Visible Tools of an Invisible Trade

"Energy is my primary tool. However, as I am a physical being, I also use tangible items that I consider the tools of my trade."

AS PHYSICAL BEINGS IN PHYSICAL BODIES, WE NEED TO USE a variety of tangible tools to express and affect the energies around us. In this chapter we will explore three of these basic tools—color, jewelry and food. I will offer exercises to assist you to be more aware of the different vibrations and frequencies of each.

Your goal is to begin to think about these physical accoutrements in new ways and to relate to them as vibrations rather than as objects, accessories or nourishment. I believe you will discover that each tool supports, enhances or contains the flow of energies in different and unique ways.

Colour as frequency
EXERCISE 1

Experiment with your choice of clothing. Try to sense/feel the appropriate color and tone for the forthcoming day. Pay attention to how it feels to be in that particular range of frequencies. If possible, change your clothes half way through an event, a meeting, your shopping expedition, or the day.

Can you sense/feel a difference? Note what you observe.

EXERCISE 2

Go into a clothing or fabric store and sense/feel the different colors, textures or patterns present there.

- Is one color cool and calming, another hot and fiery?
- Is one pattern busy and chaotic, or static and flat?
- Does one texture have more life and vibrancy?
- Is another deep, full and rich?

Run through your mind a list of adjectives so that you have words at your disposal to describe the clothing or fabrics you are exploring.

NOTES

EXERCISE 3

Buy yourself half a dozen inexpensive scarves of different colors. Take them with you as you move through your day. Pull one out when you are drawn to have that color present. Wrap it around your waist, neck or hang it from your handbag or briefcase.

Attempt to feel/sense the change that occurs just from having a particular color in your auric field. Practice. Do not expect to have full awareness from your first attempt. Be patient with yourself. You will become more skilled as you practice. Note your experiences. Record your observations.

NOTES

Jewelry as an energetic tool
EXERCISE 1

Tune into the day that lies before you—the place and the people with whom you will be interacting for a particular time frame. Intuitively choose the jewelry that is appropriate for this period. Do not put on the jewelry. Wrap it in a protective jewelry bag to take with you for the day.

Now choose one or two other pieces that are of other colors or types, or carry a different 'feeling'. Add those to your jewelry bag. Now choose your clothes for that day or time frame.

Pay attention to the colors and textures that you choose, for each contributes to the overall *energetic* effect. Yes, there is an aesthetic effect as well, but for the purpose of this exercise, you will only be focusing on the *energetic* aspect.

Go about your work, assignment or day's activities. Pay attention to how you feel, how smoothly you are able to interact. Does the flow feel easy and smooth, or do you feel like you are fighting a wave of resistance? Note this feeling.

NOW, PUT ON THE JEWELRY that you had chosen as appropriate for this time period. Feel the difference. Is there a shift? Is there an augmentation of one feeling or another? Trust that you will feel the difference.

Next, put on the alternate jewelry that you have brought with you, the pieces that were *not* chosen for this event. Put them on and sense the difference. Do you feel supported, assisted, inhibited or restrained?

Remember, I am not talking here about whether the jewelry matches the outfit that you have chosen to wear, though that too can make a difference, but rather I am calling your attention to the energetics of the circumstance—how you 'feel' with one set of choices versus another.

Make up a story if necessary of what you imagine your reaction might be. Then trust that, in fact, the fantasy is an actual reaction, you were just not tuned into it. Your intuitive reactions to this subtle realm will get stronger and you will trust them more and more as you practice. Please record your experiences and your observations here.

NOTES

EXERCISE 2

Please go into a store, café or enclosed environment and feel and experience what you sense in that space. Now, put on a pair of earrings, a ring or necklace that you have chosen ahead of time, that you felt intuitively would augment your process, magnify or diminish your energy. Again, feel and experience yourself in the energy of this environment with this different jewelry. Note any differences.

Remember, the reactions, the sense/feel of whatever you experience will be subtle. Do not expect lightning flashes or thunderclaps, though that would be fun. More likely, your insights will be as subtle as butterfly wings, as soft and gentle as a whisper.

Whatever you sense, feel, or think, *receive* it and allow it to be a truth. Each time you practice this exercise, your intuitions will get stronger and it will be easier to believe and trust.

Men, you need not feel left out of this exercise. You too can experiment with different colors, textures and accessories. I have seen a lot of very attractive pink and purple shirts recently.

As different choices change your appearance, so it will also change the frequencies that constitute your walking-around-package of energy and will ultimately alter the effect of your energetic efforts.

Enjoy this experience of dressing up. Have fun with this experiment! Record your experiences here.

NOTES

Food as a vibrational tool
EXERCISE

Review your eating habits, not to judge them but to understand your basic pattern. Each food has a different frequency. Some foods are heavy—a slow frequency— pasta, bread, potatoes, for example. Others are light—a more rapid frequency, like celery, lettuce and watermelon.

Experiment eating foods with different frequencies and try to sense/feel the different results in the energies in your body. Note what you sense/feel.

Do you tend to eat heavy foods with slower vibrations or lighter foods with faster frequencies? Try varying your diet and see if you can feel the difference in your body's energy. Record what you learn.

Review your eating history. Look back over the times in your life when your eating habits changed, whether due to stress, illness, joy, or in order to lose weight. Think back on your experience and record the energetic differences you felt from the different foods you consumed.

What about the times when you spontaneously shifted your eating habits for no apparent reason. Can you attribute the change to something going on in the unseen energetic world around you? Can you imagine that you might have been resonating to the subtle clues in the field? Record your observations.

In present time, ask yourself if certain foods are most appropriate for the coming day? Listen to your intuitive voice and note if your digestion and sense of well-being are supported by your choices. Are you more or less resonant with the population around you? Record what you sense/feel/observe.

YOU ARE INDEED WHAT YOU EAT. You are all the complexity of the frequencies and vibrations of the various foods you consume. Happy eating!

NOTES

NOTES

CHAPTER 8

A Multi-Dimensional Conversation

"Rational Mind tried to understand the intricacies of this human holiday and could not, so it let go and allowed Intuition to take over and Feeling to be present and to guide the dance. Being replaced Understanding."

"SO WHAT IS THIS ENERGY BETWEEN US?" asked *Strange Bird*, an extra-terrestrial being, stranded on planet earth, of her human companion.

"Multi-dimensional, at the least; fun at its best," the *Human* responded.

So it was that the space was filled with all the *Present Moment* could hold. The *Moment* let go of itself for just an instant and wondered,

"What is this?"

Reason sat mute, feeling the sacredness of the space.

Time and *Space* melted the past, present and future into one and imploded the whole into the divine.

"Oh, what a delicate dance this is to see,

There will be a moment when, in this space and time,

All will see, what it is TO BE."

"But, what's coming next?" asked *Present Time*.

Future said, "Stop worrying about me.

For without staying in the present, there will be no future and I will be deprived of

both my now and my then. Just be, and all will take care of itself."

Beingness jumped in and cried out,

"What does that mean?"

The *Universe* responded with a silence so full, so pregnant and so joyous that all who heard, stopped, bowed their heads in awe and allowed the stillness to penetrate their cells, fill them with radiance and then, as the light grew, they found each other and all joined hands and danced in celebration.

Future and *Beingness* knew and understood.

Future chimed in and reminded *Present* to pay attention to where she was residing, for only then could she make appropriate decisions, be authentic, and know truth.

Strange Bird asked her human counterpart,

> "Why do you wear such a bizarre costume and behave in such a weird manner?"

The *Human* responded,

> "This is the way of the human condition. It requires strength and courage to exist and be in such a strange land. Yet the learning is great—deeper and more profound than anywhere else in this planetary system. I choose to be here to accelerate my growth, to master life in a restrictive three-dimensional body, to master the expression of emotions and to learn to overcome the limits of time and space as are known here.
>
> Is it not wonderful to be here and to be provided with such a myriad of opportunities?
>
> Is it not worth being a stranger in a strange land?
>
> I am happy; no, I am ecstatic to have such a chance."

Strange Bird nodded, knowing the truth of the *Human's* sharing but feeling tired of the journey and missing her home.

> "I don't know yet where truth lies. I only know I had a few pathways cleared. This physical journey is teaching me something I need to know. That is my work. It relates to time and space and cells and knowing."

Present Time suggested that it would be nice, awfully nice, if *Future Time* were already present so that an in-person sharing could occur. *Future Time* reminded *Present Time* that sharing is taking place and can be known and felt, if one is open to it and unafraid.

Present Time nodded in assent and admitted she knew this to be true. How she knew, she didn't know,

But that she knew, she knew.

And she was glad...

Rational Mind tried to understand the intricacies of this human holiday and could not, so it let go and allowed *Intuition* to take over and feelings to be present and to guide the dance.

Being replaced *Understanding*.

The dancers spun and circled and moved forward and back and swayed to the music of the heavens until there was only one rhythm, one beat, one being.

In that moment there was understanding.

Little did they realize that *Understanding* and *Knowing* had existed all along.

> "How can I admit that learning to feel is my work?" asked *Strange Bird*.
>
> "How can we be living in such different worlds and still be so connected?"
>
> "By breathing, by feeling, by caring," whispered *Present Time* in quick response.

"Time and space are only constructs, you silly one; they don't really exist at all."

"Right," said *Rational Mind* with disgust, as she poked at the flowers to test their reality. "They are real and beautiful and they exist in one time and space and not the other."

At that moment *Future Time* intervened.
"Relax, all of you.
Be patient and watch the future unfold.
You're going to learn to melt matter,
To jump space,
To time-travel
To feel deeply.
Be patient and enjoy the process. There is much to learn and what fun it's going to be."

Then *Future* winked and chuckled as she said,
"The present is there to whet your appetite for the future.
Consider it an appetizer to a delicious meal, an incentive to make you want to unlock the still-closed doors to the mysteries of the Universe. Fear not. You will have the keys very, very soon."

Strange Bird smiled for she knew the truth of what she heard.
Trusting…
Trusting that feelings bridge those different spaces.
Trusting that the other will remember.
Trusting to stay open while trusting.
The issue below the surface of comparison and judgment is
Trust—of oneself and of the other…
Strange Bird looked around to see whom she could trust.
Because she was afraid, she didn't trust anyone.
She stayed within herself and didn't reach out or open herself to risk.
All those around her wanted to reach out to her,
To reassure her,
To make her feel safe.
She didn't let them in; she was stuck in her fear.

Then *Trust* came close, touched her gently on the cheek,
Dried her tears and handed her an iris, deep blue in color and vibrant with life.
"Hold this for courage," *Trust* said.
"See yourself in its beauty.

See yourself in my eyes," she added.

"See what I see and know yourself.

Then you will be unafraid and able to trust."

She looked into *Trust*'s eyes and saw a strange bird and knew that she had much to learn about herself. Part of her was excited and part of her was terrified.

She had learned to look *Trust* in the face,

To call her by name,

To stand firm and still.

"This is a beginning", she thought,

"The rest is yet to come!"

Strange Bird held the iris and walked across the huge expanse of space.

Patience and *Self Confidence* picked up their heads and waved their wings, trying to get someone's attention. Together they yelled,

> "Be still and listen; you're not listening to the right tones. The music of the spheres can sometimes be deafening and dulling to the senses. One must be very quiet to hear its nuances, to feel its beauty and power. Trust in one's ability to hear is paramount.
>
> If one doubts, it is likely you will miss the beat.
>
> If one believes and trusts, then the tones and pulsations, the full range of celestial colors, will be present.
>
> Open your eyes, your ears, and mostly your heart and then you'll know. It won't be long—for there is no length of time or space. It is only too long for the mind; the senses know the truth.
>
> If given half a chance to be open.
>
> You can know and feel it all."

Spirit intervened.

> "We are all multi-dimensional beings capable of many expressions at once. Do not hinder my work by your limited comprehension of what you are capable of doing.
>
> Openness and faith are everything.
>
> Remember—miracles are really commonplace.
>
> They are only labels for what you earthlings don't yet understand."

"A part of me doesn't really have a clue about what is occurring," thought *Strange Bird*, "and the other part of me knows it all.

Boy, I wish they'd get together for the dance!"

A conversation between Present Moment, Future, Space, Reason, Trust, Beingness, Patience, Confidence, Strange Bird (a multi-dimensional being newly on earth and feeling lost) and her human companion from "Songs of Strange Bird" by Elaine Seiler, 2003.

EXERCISE

For this workbook chapter your exercise is to personally explore the ideas discussed in "A Multi-Dimensional Conversation".

- Do you agree or disagree with the concepts presented?

- Where do you find yourself on the continuum between fear and trust?

- Do you live predominantly in the past, the future or the present?

- What is holding you back from moving further along the path to trust or living in the present? Are you willing to take a step?

- Take that step, write about your shift away from fear to living in trust... and describes how it feels.

NOTES

CHAPTER 9

By-Products of Energy Work

"Symptoms can also be guides to various energetic states. What some people diagnose as a 'mere cold', congestion or a bad knee ... are no longer just that. Once we enter the world of energetics there is greater significance and metaphor in these physical symptoms."

AS WE ARE ABOUT HALF WAY THROUGH THIS TRAINING WORKBOOK, I trust you are becoming more and more comfortable with the energy world. You have learned to recognize an energetic field, to understand its subtle language, to pinpoint the different jobs that you may be doing and to identify your particular sensitivities or capabilities in the energy world. In this chapter we will explore the reactions you may have as your body acts as an energetic instrument of change.

Sometimes when the work is extreme, when the situation is very toxic, when the demand is very great or the body is physically or energetically depleted, I experience ailments that seem to be mine and seem to be physical, but are actually a reflection of the field and are primarily energetic. They are the physical by-products of an energetic stimulus.

For example, I often become congested, when the environment in which I am working is 'congested'. We will look at more examples as we proceed, but first, it is essential to distinguish whether your reactions or symptoms are physical or energetic?

EXERCISES

Exercise 1

Are your symptoms physical or energetic?

Ask yourself the following questions:

- Are the symptoms constant, consistent and moving along a rational path or are they erratic and ever changing? If the latter, they are most likely energetic.

- Is your imbalance reflecting an emotional state of disharmony? For example... is your nose running and are your eyes weeping for the loss of life from the recent earthquake? If so, there is a good likelihood that the symptom is energetic.

In your mind, review the last time you were ill or out of balance.
- Can you recall what was occurring in the field at that time?
- Were there any natural disasters in the news?
- Were there any emotional upheavals in your personal life?

IF SO, PLEASE CONSIDER whether your so-called 'illness' is truly the result of a virus or a bacteria or if it might be a reflection or expression of whatever imbalance was in the field.

NOTES

Exercise 2

Are you aging or being?

Check your thoughts the next time you hear yourself denying your youth or bemoaning your age. Be aware that your thoughts are affecting the energies of your body; they are affecting the aging process.

Do you ever think, "I am getting old; my hair is turning gray" or do you ever blame your bloated belly on your increasing years? When you think or speak those thoughts you are reinforcing the aging process.

Pay attention to your thoughts and statements. During the coming week note all your thoughts re your body and the aging process. Write them here so you can really see how you are influencing your reality.

NOTES

Exercise 3
Coping with fatigue

- Is this fatigue physical or energetic?
- Is this my fatigue or another's?
- Is my fatigue associated with a particular environment or group?
- Is my support of a place or group of people draining my energies?
- Are there metaphors present in the situation that can help me interpret what is occurring energetically?

Please record your observations.

NOTES

CHAPTER 10

Blended State

"In the blended state, I was learning to encompass in my body and my energy field, the characteristics of both the physical and subtle realms."

IN THIS CHAPTER I WILL DESCRIBE THE CHARACTERISTICS of the blended state. I will then offer some exercises to help you to identify the unique qualities of this state and assist you to recognize when you are in it.

First, let us review. I have previously identified several stages in the process of humankind's movement from a three-dimensional to an other-dimensional consciousness.

Stage One: Awakening

Humankind gradually begins to remove the blinders from their consciousness about life, about what is real and what is not. Intuition and psychic abilities increase.

Stage Two: Bridge State

Individual vibrations speed up. Sensitivities to the world beyond the three dimensions are heightened. Extra-sensory perceptions are increased. The individual lives with one foot in each dimensional realm.

Stage Three: Blended State

We will examine the characteristics of the blended state below.

Stage Four: Fourth Dimension

Humans retain their physical bodies, but in a less dense, less individualized way.

Final Stage:

Finally, humans will fully reside in the other or higher dimensions.

LET'S NOW LOOK IN DEPTH AT THE CHARACTERISTICS of the blended state.

Physical world as perceived from the blended state

- The physical world is still physical, but it is less dense.
- The ordinary rules of physicality no longer apply in the same way.
- Boundaries are energetic, not physical; space is bound by energy, not form.
- Distance can be shortened or lengthened by thought intention.
- Appearances are deceiving. Things are not what they seem to be.
- Bi-location (being in two places at once) and morphing (shape shifting) are options. Invisibility is more possible.
- Blended beings feel invisible and are less visible to others. The more blended they become, the less physically present they are.
- They are not part of the collective consciousness while working energetically in other dimensions.
- New physical systems may be needed in order to align with the new blended energy.
- Physical protection is not as necessary as it is in the physical world. One is protected by one's knowingness.
- The body may reside physically in one place; the essence of the blended being may be energetically elsewhere.
- The world of time does not exist in the same way as in prior states.
- A traditional timeframe no longer applies. Energy activity is done 24/7.

Physical body as perceived from the blended state

- The physical body is less dense.
- The wider the range of frequencies in the body, the better equipped a blended being is to work in the energetic realms.
- The body gives fewer clear signals, for example it is less likely to indicate hunger or thirst. Some physical responses are more immediate—congestion or vertigo from a toxic environment; others responses are more delayed—pain, fatigue or muscular aches are often felt hours after exertion.
- Healing responses change. The body doesn't respond to physical remedies as it once did.
- Sensitivities are enhanced. Psychic awareness is enormously increased. Synchronicities and telepathy are more frequent. Knowingness is more present.

- Physical ailments are now perceived as energetic reflections.
- Less sleep is needed by blended beings. The body rejuvenates in less time.
- Memory skills are diminished, not due to age but due to the effect of being mostly energetic.
- Motor-neuron patterns are altered (small motor skills may be difficult to *control)*.

Emotional body as perceived from the blended state

- Emotions are more balanced.
- There is a greater acceptance of what is.
- Confidence in one's knowingness grows over time.
- Blended beings connect electrically and energetically, more than emotionally to other beings.
- Sexual and gender identification are more blurred. This is a reflection of the lessening of polarity in the blended state.

Values as perceived from the blended state

- The values that guide actions are primarily energetic rather than personal, familial, cultural, social, aesthetic, ethical, political or economic.
- Ingenuity and intuition are more available and effective than rational interpretation.
- Group mind exists; it supersedes individuality.
- Collaboration, inclusiveness, unity, integrity and accountability prevail as a result of shared consciousness.
- Truth telling is essential. Speaking the shadow removes its power.
- Acting as if, is not good enough. All must, in fact, be in alignment.

Dreams as perceived from the blended state

- Dreams are enactments of a real process.
- Dreams occur in another dimension, not in the physical world and not in linear time.

Communication as perceived from the blended state

- Communication becomes more energetic.
- Communication between blended and non-blended beings becomes more and more challenging as one gets more and more blended.
- Words don't easily traverse the veil between the physical and the energetic worlds.
- A new language using metaphor, symbol and descriptive story-telling must be found.

Characteristics of a blended state of consciousness

- One holds a clear attitudinal 'yes', rather than, 'yes, but'.
- One's consciousness is expanded, one's perceptions wider.
- Attitudes are collaborative, not divisive.
- Trust, not fear, rules.
- Positive attitudes reign.
- Egos are put aside and the goal is the catalyzing force.
- Interaction is based on truth and integrity.
- A non-denominational spirituality is the guide.
- Stewardship of the earth and her resources is the way.
- Win/win solutions are the norm.
- One knows, not hopes, that success is possible.
- The field one holds creates the reality one desires.
- Reality is non-linear and non-polarized.
- A commitment to abundance overrides the concept of scarcity.
- An attitude of gratitude fuels manifestation.

EXERCISE

For these questions, please focus on the present or recent past. Reflect on whether there have been any subtle changes in your body, emotions, sense of time or space, or your values and indicate how you know. You might also want to identify any changes you have noticed since you started reading this book. Please make notes in the spaces provided regarding the following.

- Are your senses heightened, your perceptions more keen?

- Has your sense of space and time shifted?

- Have you added any foods to your diet to increase the range of your frequencies?

- Are you more or less responsive to those around you?

- Can you identify when you are no longer in a strictly three-dimensional reality?

- What makes you say that you are in a bridge or blended state?

- Has your sleep pattern changed? To what do you attribute that change?

- Have you altered your language, expanding your choice of words and metaphors?

- Have you experienced any so-called illnesses or symptoms? How do you perceive them now?

- Review your sense of time, has it changed or altered?

- Have you experienced any unusual shifts in your emotions? Are your moods more even, more irregular, higher or lower?

- What things appear to be one way and are really another?

- What have you manifested recently? Was that manifestation easier and more simultaneous than you have experienced in earlier times? Did you feel the process was different in any way?

- Consider whether your recent experiences feel the same or different from previous similar situations? To what do you attribute those differences?

NOTES

NOTES

CHAPTER 11

Midwife to the Stars

"Beings from beyond the veil crossed the dimensional divide. These hitchhikers from the galaxy were able to take on physical form through my energetic wombing."

IN THIS CHAPTER, I DESCRIBE ONE OF THE MORE UNUSUAL JOBS that I have done as an energy worker... that of being the bridge, connection or the equivalent of a womb space for other-dimensional beings coming onto the earth without going through the birth canal or regular gestation process.

I have found innumerable coins and been told they were multi-dimensional beings. I have seen ethereal insects which were also beings coming onto the planet for the first time. I have had bumps, bites, pimples and pulled muscles that were my body's physical reaction to the temporary energetic presence of an other-dimensional being, using my body as a transit zone or womb space, to gather enough material presence so they could then take on full physicality in whatever form they chose. I believe this is possible.

The exercise in this section is a series of questions geared to opening your awareness and seeding new ideas. I understand that these ideas may be challenging to accept. If that is so for you, no problem! Merely note what you believe below. I suggest you date these remarks, so you can track any changes in your attitudes that occur over time.

EXERCISE

- Have you ever found a series of coins—not just one coin, but several, one after another in unexpected places in a given time period? At the time you may have thought this rather odd, but now can you imagine that each of these coins might be a disembodied being, trying to come into form in the three- dimensional world? Describe your experience, what you thought then and what you think now.

- What about other unusual repeated experiences? Have you found numerous feathers or shells or had repeated encounters with specific animals? What do you think these experiences indicated?

- Have you ever experienced a skin blemish or bump that came and went in such a way that you suspected it was not a typical skin condition? At the time, you had no idea what it might have been. Now, what do you think is possible?

- Have you ever experienced a miracle of healing? What occurred? Why do you believe it was a miracle?

- Have you ever had 'training dreams' in which you were in a schoolroom or conference center? In these dreams, did you see or just sense the presence of those you were training or those by whom you were being trained?

- Is it possible that you were sharing your physical world with unseen other-dimensional beings?

- Have you ever looked at an insect or animal and had the surprising thought that you were encountering an *other-dimensional being*? What made you say this, even if only to yourself?

- Have you ever seen, in your mind's eye, a creature you *knew* was not a three-dimensional, earth-based being? You *knew* that the being was real, but it appeared imaginary. Ask for some guidance from your personal guides about that being and be willing to hear the response.

NOTES

NOTES

CHAPTER 12

Multi-Dimensional Partnering

"My future partner was to be a being from another dimension. He was not in-body at that time, but would come into body shortly and would be my energetic partner."

IN THE THIRD DIMENSION, WE ARE ACCUSTOMED TO traditional partnerships of physical men and women, men and men and women and women in intimate, social and professional relationships in all variations. There are, however, other VERY unusual partnerships that exist, that are quite real energetically, but do not show up as typical physical interactions. In Chapter 12, I describe my very unusual experience of sensing a possible intimate partnership with a being from the other side of the veil. This being had physicality only by overshadowing a physical human. I refer to this being as an 'overshadow'.

For those of you who are familiar with the concept of a walk-in or a being who walks into a physical body and changes places with the original inhabiting soul, the overshadow is a very different unfolding. An overshadow co-habits with the original physical person in the body. They merge and become one. They join in this way to enable the original soul to remain in-body and receive the gift of an in-flow of higher energies and to facilitate the other-dimensional being's ability to do a job that requires his special skills on the planet. To do this job, he needs a physical body. He could not afford the time to go through the ordinary birth and maturation process. His job had to be done at that time.

I encountered such a being in 1999 and felt his presence strongly and deeply until he withdrew back into the other dimensions in 2002. My connection to him was strong, intense, visceral, and felt totally truthful. I felt a soul-level and personal connection to this overshadow being. At first I resisted such a strange notion, but over time, I allowed myself to engage with both the physical being and the essence of the overshadowing soul. I trusted that my sensing of this being or my intuitive knowing of him was real, though there was no material proof of his presence.

I invite you to imagine, if not fully believe, that such unusual partnering does, in fact, occur. Have you had similar experiences? Please describe them here.

If you have had a similar experience please email me at elaine@multi-dimensionalyou.com. There is so little written on this type of experience that I would greatly appreciate hearing what you have to share on this subject.

NOTES

THERE ARE OTHER MULTI-DIMENSIONAL and energetic partnerings that are important to note. These need not be intimate encounters as described above, but are true energetic sharings between beings in-body and/or beings out-of-body. I am referring here to the chance encounter with a stranger on a bus or a subway. Few or no words are exchanged, but the energetic exchange is felt. It might be a sense of perfect resonance and alignment or a fleeting experience of being totally and completely seen and acknowledged. It might be a momentary association that assisted you to harmonize a space, clear out some highly toxic energy or bring light to a dark and heavy place in or outside yourself or them. The form or purpose of these energetic partnerings are many. I hope you will begin to be alert to their presence in your life and honor the gifts they bring.

Enjoy your partnerings of whatever sort they may be, whether fully physical or totally energetic or some unexpected combination of both. There is no telling how a partnering will manifest in your life. Try not to limit your expectation in terms of gender, race or type of being.

EXERCISE

Pick a day or an outing or a period of time for this exercise. During this time, set an intention of observing and participating in the energetic exchanges that unfold. Now go forth and observe.

Watch for the unspoken exchange that occurs through the eyes. Watch for the stranger who asks a question, engages with you for a moment and then goes his way.

Watch for the messages hidden in the words of someone on the street, or in the supermarket checkout line.

Observe your reactions to things that might have gone unnoticed except for this exercise and its intention. For example, you might be on a checkout line sharing with a friend your latest passion for animation, when the person in front of you offers you the name and address of one of the most skilled practitioners in the field. Sounds too good to be true! I witnessed this occurrence.

Watch for leads, links, clues, messages, inspiration and guidance in all its guises. Watch for partners who come in and out of your life in a fleeting, but absolutely critical moment. Then make notes of your experiences and enjoy the thrill of recognizing and appreciating those moments and those partners.

NOTES

CHAPTER 13

Dream Interpretation: a Multi-Dimensional Perspective

"From a metaphysical perspective, a dream is a true energetic state during which a real experience occurs for both the physical dreamer and the energetic beings that are involved."

IN THIS CHAPTER, WE WILL EXPLORE THE CONCEPT OF multi-dimensional dream interpretation, in which dreams are considered real events occurring in a different plane of reality. The focus in this perspective is on the information about the other dimensions or the interactions between the other dimensions and this physical reality. There may also be psychological, emotional and symbolic interpretations of these dreams, but those will be backgrounded for our process here.

For example, if you dream, as I did, about being embraced and kissed in three different ways by three different men, allow that this dream might be a training for non-physical beings in the different kinds of touches that exist in the physical world, rather than a psychological analysis of my social skills with men.

Of, if you dream of a conference center in which a myriad of different classes are being held, consider this a real event held for the benefit of disembodied beings, rather than a symbolic procedure with hidden meanings.

If you want to analyze your dreams in the traditional way, feel free to do so. Please also interpret your dreams from an energetic or multi-dimensional perspective. Give yourself the opportunity to delve into the reality of the other realms as well as the one in which you have lived in and know so well.

EXERCISE

At the beginning of this workbook, I suggested that you note all the dreams you have had while doing these exercises. Now is the time to attempt to interpret them from this new and enlightening multi-dimensional perspective. The following questions will assist you to see the bigger picture in your dreams, beyond the words and the scenes depicted. Ask yourself the following questions as you review and interpret your dreams.

- What do you sense is taking place underneath the physical description?

- What metaphors are present in your dreams that offer clues to this larger reality?

- Is there *magic* present? Might that indicate movement beyond the veil of physicality? From this new perspective what have you discovered?

- Try to sense/feel beyond the material images of the physical dream world to those that might be present in the energetic dream realm. Share what you discover.

BE WILLING TO TAKE A LEAP of *knowing* across the bridge that separates and unites the world of physicality and the world of energy. I hope you have fun interpreting your dreams.

NOTES

NOTES

CHAPTER 14

Creating a Multi-Dimensional Business

"A multi-dimensional business reflects the characteristics and values of the other dimensions. Such a venture may look ordinary, but it is not. It is not restricted by polarized concepts, time or form."

EVERY DAY MILLIONS OF PEOPLE AROUND THE GLOBE engage in businesses and projects, for profit and not-for-profit ventures. For the most part, these enterprises are third-dimensional in nature. They focus on producing, promoting and selling physical goods and services to their clients. There is little concern for the energies that weave in and out of these ventures that effect their every movement, their success or their failures. In the parallel chapter in the companion book, "Multi-Dimensional YOU", I share the story of my experience creating a sustainable agriculture business in Australia. I will not repeat that tale here. Suffice it to say, that I learned a great deal.

As one moves along the evolutionary pathways and one's frequencies become more and more rapid, the old ways of conducting business cease to work or cease to function easily and smoothly. New guidelines are essential. These guidelines or principles can be applied to creating a business, attracting a partner, initiating a project, increasing your income, or manifesting a new home. The key ingredients are clarity, integrity, alignment and resonance. And, each step requires an awareness of the energies present in each participant and in the group as a whole. In the next chapter I will delve into the guidelines or what I call the "Sixteen Commandments of Multi-Dimensional Manifestation". Before I reveal those ingredients, I would like you to do one short exercise in order to set the stage or the context for what is about to be revealed.

EXERCISE

Take a few moments to review a project, venture or business, for profit or not-for-profit, large or small with which you are involved today. Specifically look at the values and beliefs that underlie the venture. List them below and note whether they are based on physical third-dimensional reality or whether they contain an awareness of the energetic, unseen world. For example, is there constant talk and focus on the financial bottom line? Is there concern with harmony and teamwork? Is there an awareness of the unseen forces that interplay with the physical reality which must be dealt with each and every day?

That is all you need to do at this moment. Just increase your awareness of what *is*.

In the next chapter you will learn the essential ingredients of manifestation as I understand it and can compare what has been, to what is required in the newly evolving world.

NOTES

CHAPTER 15

Manifestation in a Multi-Dimensional World

"Traditional guidelines for manifestation in the three-dimensional world are not enough to ensure manifestation once one has begun the process of energetic evolution."

IN THIS SECTION, WE ARE GOING TO LOOK IN DEPTH at what I call the Sixteen Commandments of Multi-Dimensional Manifestation. I believe these principles are necessary to manifest one's goals in the newly evolving world.

Commandments One through **Ten** are traditionally applied in the third dimension.

Commandment One

Set a clear intention.

State that intention as a positive affirmation, in present time, as if it already exists, for it does exist in the energetic realms where all thoughts begin and all things are possible. It can then be brought from the energetic realm into manifested form. Be very careful how you state your goal.

Affirmation: *I hold an unshakeable commitment to my intention and its manifestation. My intention is manifested now.*

Commandment Two

Ensure that your beliefs are in alignment with your goals.

Sometimes we aim high, but do not believe we deserve the very things we seek. If we are self-critical or judgmental that judgment subtly shapes the manifested goal.

Affirmation: *All my beliefs are in perfect alignment with my intentions.*

Commandment Three

Ensure that your values support your intention.

All values surrounding a project must be in alignment. If you seek to be of service to your customers while your business partner is only seeking a profit, your success may be impeded by this lack of harmony of intention.

If you seek a new house to give your family a healthy comfortable place to live, but you really don't believe that you deserve to live in such a wonderful situation, it will be exceedingly difficult for you to manifest the home you seek. It is necessary to probe your conscious and unconscious values.

Affirmation: *My values support the perfect manifestation of my goal.*

Commandment Four

Hold an unshakeable commitment.

Such a commitment means that you will steadfastly hold the focus on your goal, no matter how long it takes, no matter the effort it requires.

Affirmation: *I put my passion and full commitment behind the manifestation of my goal.*

Commandment Five

Build a solid foundation.

Every stone in that foundation must be properly positioned and aligned with every other, so that the building will not sway, fall, tilt or require shoring up further down the road.

Affirmation: *My intentions are fully supported by the underlying structure and systems that express and guide them.*

Commandment Six

Take all necessary physical steps to follow through to the goal.

We are physical beings, learning and adopting energetic principles. It's therefore essential that we follow through physically as well as energetically, as we seek to manifest change in our lives.

Affirmation: *I clearly sense and take each and every step required to reach my goal.*

Commandment Seven

Release all toxicity.

Addictions, substance abuse, an over-inflated ego or an inability to change are all toxic and antithetical to manifestation. Energetically, they interrupt movement. They are as real and substantive as physical blockages, for in the energy world, they exist! They literally stop movement, force our energies away from the intended goal, divert and sap attention.

As we let go and release these toxicities, the energies of the other dimensions are able to flow through us and the new desired goals can actualize. We then become conduits for the change we seek.

As physical humans beings become more and more energetically aware and connected to the other dimensions, we are required to be more exact and diligent in the physical world. Every action must be more carefully executed. We are becoming more sensitive, not less; we must become more responsible, not less.

Affirmation: *I release all toxicity and hold my energetic and physical being to be pristine.*

Commandment Eight

Observe and respond to the metaphors and subtle reflective messages in the field.

The language of energy is subtle but clear. As we learned in the chapter, "Language of Energy", energy speaks to us through the climatic conditions of nature, the comfort or discomfort of our bodies, synchronicity and coincidences as well as through the metaphors present in dreams and in our waking lives if we will but look.

What might it mean if you have a 'stiff' neck or a 'bloated' stomach or a compulsion to speak all the time? What might you learn about yourself and your goal if you stopped to reflect on the metaphors you identify?

Affirmation: *I am aware of the project's metaphors and reflections in the larger field. I successfully intuit the messages from the subtle realms.*

Commandment Nine

Express gratitude for all you have. Be in-joy.

The expression of appreciation changes one's vibration and catalyzes the manifestation of one's desires.

Affirmation: *I experience joy, appreciation and gratitude in every aspect of the manifestation of this goal.*

Commandment Ten

Demand excellence and integrity in all aspects of moving towards your goal.

Once you begin to evolve towards a more energetic way of being in the world, the Universe will only support responsibility, integrity and accountability. This seems to be true no matter what your goal, a new house, partner or business. The energy requirements are similar and must be at a high level.

Affirmation: *I require excellence and integrity in all aspects of my project. I elicit and depend on the creative and ethical contributions of everyone involved.*

COMMANDMENTS ONE TO TEN are physically based commandments. They are essential for manifestation in the three-dimensional world. They are however, not enough to ensure manifestation once one has begun the process of energetic evolution. Once you cross what I like to refer to as the energetic divide, you need to be aware of and follow an additional six commandments in order to efficiently manifest as a blended or multi-dimensional being.

As we humans become more and more blended, we become less and less grounded in the third dimension, less and less able to function as ordinary three-dimensional beings. Manifestation becomes more difficult. This was surprising to me as I thought that the more energetic I became, the easier it would be to manifest my goals. Not true!

To be an energetic attractor, which is how three-dimensional beings magnetize their goals, we must have within our beingness, a broad range of frequencies that are only available in the physical realm. Once we become predominantly blended, we are energetically lighter and have a more rapid, but smaller range of frequencies than the average physical being. We appear dense and physical, but in reality we are not. We are a package of vibrations moving very rapidly through space and time, more rapidly than we have ever moved before, so rapidly that we don't hold within us enough substance to magnetize what we seek.

If an average person holds within their beingness, hypothetically, eight hundred frequencies, we, in our more evolved fully blended states, now hold only eighty or one hundred. In the energetic realms all those extra frequencies are not needed because there is much more resonance, alignment and oneness between the beings in that realm. That unanimity ensures almost instant manifestation. However, in the blended state in the still physical world, there isn't enough substance in those reduced number of frequencies to draw to us what we are trying to attract. We need assistance from the other dimensional realms. That assistance acts as a substitute for the frequencies that we are lacking.

This is where **Commandments Eleven to Sixteen**, the multi-dimensional commandments come into play.

Commandment Eleven

Ensure the energetic alignment of all people and aspects of the unfolding of the goal.

Everyone involved in the manifestation of the goal must be in alignment with the intention. If even one person steps out of the energetic circle, the energy falters; the timetable slows down and the path is diverted. Then, twice the energy is required to bring all the players back in line again.

Affirmation: *Every part of my goal is in perfect alignment with every other. I am aware of any imbalance in the field and intuitively know how to adjust it.*

Commandment Twelve

Create an energetic throughway from you to your goal and keep it constantly open.

The energetic path from you to your goal is as real as the physical path. Ignore either and you will flounder. You must be vigilant about both. If you sense/feel that the energies are stuck, visualize them flowing freely like a river. Intuit where they are blocked and if possible, remove the physical challenges.

Then send energy to the places, aspects or people where the vibrations seem weak. Just focusing in this way will improve the situation. Ask for assistance from your guides to build up the energies where they are faltering.

Affirmation: *The invisible path or energetic throughway from the other dimensions to the tangible physical realms is open, clear and constantly reinvigorated. To keep that path active and alive, I support every aspect of the whole to function at the highest frequency of which it is capable.*

Commandment Thirteen

Vigilantly claim your knowingness.

We, humans, have not been taught to honor our intuitive knowing. Rather we are taught to discount what is not a known or proven fact.

As we move into a blended state and a multi-dimensional world, we must relearn what we knew as small children. We must trust and honor the 'wee small voice within', the fleeting knowing that we need to turn right not left, the subtle message that a given individual is not to be trusted or the sudden knowing that a cyclone is coming and we must take our family and evacuate the house now.

Failure to listen to any of these messages could be dangerous if not fatal. . Begin today to practice listening to the wee small voice within.

Affirmation: *I know what is right and appropriate. I trust myself, and my guidance. I am guided at each step and each juncture.*

Commandment Fourteen

Acknowledge the polarity that exists in the physical world.

It's important to be aware that both the negative and positive poles are always present in the third dimension. To manifest an intention from a multi-dimensional state, we must intend the positive goal, while being aware of the negative possibility.

Affirmation: *I totally commit myself to my goal, while at the same time recognizing that its opposite exists. I affirm that it does not exist in the reality that I am creating.*

Commandment Fifteen

Ask for and accept help from the other dimensions.

Source, our angels, or guides, those beings on the other side of the veil, who care for and work with us, can and will channel to and through us, the frequencies we need. To achieve this we must call on them and ask that they help us to manifest our goals. We must do everything in our power to stay focused on our goals in as many *physical* and concrete ways as are possible.

At a certain point in the evolutionary process, we have gone or will go too far across the veil to manifest in the material world by ourselves. We will have become too energetic. Our range of frequencies will be too limited.

We need assistance from beyond the physical reality. Ironically, it's the immaterial beings on the other side of the veil that are now able to offer us the most help in manifesting in the material world.

Affirmation: *I request and accept guidance and support from the other- dimensional realms to ensure the perfect manifestation of my goals.*

Commandment Sixteen

Allow for universal alignment when creating a timeline for your goal.

While we think we know what is in the best interest of a person, a project or the planet, from the meta-perspective, that may not be so. An individual or a group may have unseen lessons still to be learned.

Certain situations not evident to our limited human understanding may still need to occur, before a particular event or experience can unfold. Sometimes, we are greatly frustrated while waiting. And, then suddenly, when universal alignment is achieved, success will be manifest.

Affirmation: *I affirm that my goal will be manifest in the perfect timing for me, for the planet and for the Universe.*

OK. LET'S PRACTICE.

Please take some time to review your efforts at manifestation from the past few years so that you can monitor your progress as you move forward. This assessment is not to swell your head with your success or make you feel badly because you thought you failed.

The following exercises have been created to assist you in evaluating your ability to attract and to manifest so that you will have greater awareness and success in the future.

Understanding the Sixteen Commandments of Manifestation

EXERCISE 1.
Taking stock

- Choose a goal you sought to manifest from a recent or current time period.

- Assess your intentions, really look at them. Were or are they are in alignment with the goal you listed?

- Now assess your beliefs. Were or are they in alignment with your stated goal? For example, if you are aiming to have your manuscript accepted by a publisher, do you believe your material is good enough to be published or does your hidden belief that you have poor writing skills undermine your goal? Do you believe in yourself enough to allow your dreams to come true?

- Assess your values. Were, or are they clear and harmonious with your goals? Do profit or service underlay the goal for your business venture? Is integrity a key project or business value? Are all your values in alignment with your goal?

- Are all the values, beliefs and intentions of all staff members, consultants or volunteer participants in alignment with the goals of the project?

- Was your commitment unshakeable or did you get pulled off course by setbacks, challenges or opposition?

- What sort of ground or foundation did you create to support your intentions? What steps did you take to ensure that you manifested your goal?

- Did you follow through to the end, physically and emotionally, or lose interest and passion and slack off on the work required to attract your desired result?

- Where you failed, might toxicity have been a contributing factor? What specific toxicity was at play here? How did it affect the goal?

- Was every person involved in the manifestation process in alignment with the goal?

- Were you aware of and did you heed the messages of the subtle metaphors present in the everyday world around you as you attempted to reach your goal?

- Did you experience joy, appreciation and gratitude for the work you were doing or that which you were experiencing?

- Was there an energetic throughway or open flow of energy between you and your goal? If not, what could you have done to release the blockage?

- Were all participants on the same page? Did they understand how they were blocking the energy, if they were?

- Were there other factors that seemed to be standing in the way? What were the blocks? What could you have done to remove the energetic and/or physical boulders?

- Did you trust your guidance/ your knowingness? Do you and did you follow that 'wee small voice inside' or did you override the voice and allow yourself to be moved off your true path?

- Did you commit yourself to your goal even while acknowledging that the opposite of what you desired could come about?

- Did you ask for assistance from the Universe, from your guides, from the angelic realm, from whomever you relate to in the realms beyond the physical?

- Do you feel you received the assistance and support you wanted and needed? If not, what do you think occurred?

- Timing is critical. Was the manifestation of your goal easy and rapid or was the timing off and it seemingly took forever? In retrospect can you now see that perhaps it was not yet time for whatever you sought to manifest? Universal timing is not always the same as personal timing.

EXERCISE 2
Taking stock, a second experience

Now repeat the exercise with a different experience in mind. If you used a goal with a successful conclusion in the first part of this exercise, try again but now focus on an experience in which you were frustrated and felt like you were not succeeding.

If you focused in EXERCISE 1 on a so-called failure, now focus on an experience where you manifested what you desired. See what you can learn from your past process so that you can manifest more easily and consistently in the future.

NOTES

EXERCISE 3
Goal manifestation

- Set yourself a brand new goal or commit yourself to something you have deeply desired and are passionate about. Affirm your intention and commitment.

- Spell out the values and beliefs that underlie this intention. Probe deeply to ensure that you are truly in harmony with what you state you are seeking.

- Enumerate the steps to be taken to that goal with clear and manageable timelines. Be very clear about the aspects that will form the foundation on which all else rests.

- Share that strategy and those guidelines with a trusted friend in order to make them tangible and real.

- Take each physical step, one at a time, while creating an energetic pathway on which to tread that will help you move from wherever you are to where you seek to go. To create such an energetic throughway, visualize it and trust that the energy of that visualization is as real as a physical roadway.

- Periodically repeat the visualization, seeing the goal manifested in all its aspects to ensure that the energy of manifestation continues to flow from you to the goal.

- As you seek your goal, check out your attachment to the way the goal will manifest. Let go to the Universe and trust that you will be cared for and that the Universe *will* respond... even if it is in what might be a totally unexpected manner. Declare your commitment to universal not personal timing. While you are aware of the challenges you face, hold strongly to *your knowing* that the goal you desire is attainable. Affirm your knowing.

- Step back from your life and look at it objectively, as if from a distance, where you have great clarity. Explore the metaphors you observe as you move step by step towards your goal. Share what you observe with a friend or partner. Listen to the words you use as you describe them, for hidden in those words are the messages from the subtle realms. Make notes below on the metaphors you discovered and your interpretations of them.

- In order to move from the ego-based three-dimensional state of consciousness to a more blended state of being, you must be willing *to look clearly*, to give up self-judgment and self-criticism. What was, was! This is a new moment. You can start now to be the person you want to be! As you look carefully, is everything in alignment? If not, what needs to be changed or adjusted?

- Is there enjoyment in all your efforts? Even when the work is challenging and the effort intense, there should be joy and satisfaction. If not, you are going against, not with, the energies of the Universe and you need to reconsider your process.

YOU ARE ON YOUR WAY TO BECOMING someone who can truly manifest his/her goals… a clear instrument of change.

NOTES

CHAPTER 16

Fourth-Dimensional State

"I am less physical than I have ever been. I still have a body but it is less dense. My vibrations are faster than ever before."

AT THIS POINT IN THE JOURNEY THROUGH THIS WORKBOOK you may be in the middle of your process of evolution. Your frequencies have sped up and your vibrations have become lighter and lighter. As this was occurring, I imagine you have had or are having some different and unusual experiences. I certainly did.

What follows are a series of questions to focus your attention of those unique experiences and assist you to identify when you have crossed through the veil and moved into the other dimensions.

Your first stop on the other side of the veil is what I refer to as the *fourth dimension*, but remember the number is not important and the location is neither exact nor physical. It is a state of being in which you remain physical, but your vibratory pattern is faster than it has been in the past.

You may find that you experience some of what is mentioned below, but not all or you may experience some of the following for a while and then slip back and not have these experiences again for weeks. There is no fixed pattern for the evolution on which you are embarking. Your pattern will be uniquely your own.

EXERCISE

- What experiences have you had that could not be validated by your ordinary senses?

- What is your current sleep pattern? Has it become erratic? Is your day a twenty-four hour cycle with little difference between day and night?

- What sort of changes are you experiencing in your identity? Is it beginning to blur, to lose its definition?

- Are you experiencing a subtle kind of merging with those around you, not in a psychologically dysfunctional way, but rather as a kind of energetic harmonic? Please explain.

- Please describe anything you have heard, sensed or felt but that you do not feel was actually present in your reality? Why do you believe it was in another dimension?

- Please talk about the process of manifestation as you are now experiencing it. Is it harder or easier to manifest your goals, despite your deep understanding of the guidelines for manifestation?

- List the experiences you have had that seem unsolvable with physical remedies. They seem to require something more, something energetic. Please explain.

ANY OF THESE SITUATIONS may indicate your movement into the 'other' dimensions, where you are more and more energetic, while retaining your physical body.

NOTES

NOTES

CHAPTER 17

Who is in Charge?

"My prior hierarchical belief that God guided the guides who guided me is not correct. I now understand, no one is in charge; everyone is."

IN THIS CHAPTER I EXPLORE THE CONCEPT OF CONSCIOUSNESS and responsibility from the other dimensional perspective. I invite you to join me in this new way of looking at what we have traditionally called *God* or the *All That Is*.

In the third dimension, there is individual knowing or consciousness, as well as collective knowing or consensus. They both exist, but they are separate. From this perspective we have projected outside of us power and knowledge that we do not have onto guides, angels and God.

In the other dimensions, consciousness is collective. That collective consciousness uses harmonics, frequencies or vibrations, to communicate to us. We on the physical side of the veil interpret what we perceive as guidance from God or other higher spiritual beings.

Though guides do have a signature vibration, they are not really beings; nor are they absolute. They can't be in charge of what happens in our lives for they are processes, translators, channels or conduits. Guides offer to those with whom they work, whatever information is needed as an energetic configuration appropriate to that moment in time and space. That energetic signature shows up in physicality as words, thoughts, ideas and concepts.

What is needed is not determined hierarchically, as it seems. The input is rather a compilation and assessment of all the energies present. No one is in charge —not the guides, not God.

I have come to understand that the energies of everyone and everything participate in the process that produces the information perceived by humankind to be God or All That Is. All those who guide—psychics, channels, spiritual gurus, enlightened humans and out-of-body guides—pull in a wide range of vibratory pieces of information, assimilate and assess them and offer a response. Their range of perception, awareness and consciousness, or knowing from the other dimensions, is far greater than ours in the third, or even in the blended state, so it appears to us that they know more than we know. In reality, they have a greater ability to tune into a larger range of frequencies and therefore, they seemingly know more.

I am not saying there is, or is not, a God or that there are, or are not, guides. I am suggesting that there is a complex process occurring that we humans have not fully recognized or acknowledged. Viewed from our limited, polarized, hierarchical three-dimensional perspective, we have projected a reality outside and above ourselves, rather than inside. In a multi-dimensional world we are like the God we have set on high. So... back to the question.

Who is in charge? We are! Each and every one of us! We are each creating our reality every moment of every day, and together we create the world around us.

EXERCISE

I invite you to explore your beliefs. Ask yourself, "Who do I believe is in charge?"

As you have expanded your viewpoint and moved from a three-dimensional to a multi-dimensional or energetic perspective, have you shifted your understanding of who is in charge? Note your current viewpoint.

AS YOU COME TO THE END OF THIS WORKBOOK observe the changes in your thinking as you progressed through the chapters and the exercises. Are you more comfortable with the esoteric and energetic? I hope so. Are you more self-confident and more trusting of that wee small voice within? What other changes have you noticed?

As a final exercise, please make some notes on where you are in your thinking about energy, energetics, and evolution as compared to when you started this exploration.

NOTES

NOTES

CHAPTER 18

The End: The Beginning

"Jump into your own unchartered territory, your own seeming void of knowingness. Walk forward on your evolutionary path trusting that you will know the next most appropriate steps, believing that the language of the subtle realms will be comprehensible to you, even though you know not how."

IF YOU WERE SUCCESSFUL IN THE PRIOR CHAPTERS, you have begun to identify the changes that have taken place in your life. You are hopefully, aware of what is occurring in *your* life from an energetic perspective and you sit comfortably with that. Your former beliefs, as you have probably experienced, have little to do with what unfolds as you and your world changes and evolves.

My hope and intention is that you are awake to the concepts described in this book. When something unusual occurs, you can say to yourself, "I am not alone. I know there are others experiencing some variation of this situation." I hope you will be comforted knowing that you are not the only one facing the shifts, whatever they may be.

I hope that you have come to put greater trust in that wee small voice inside you. I wish that I could speak with each and every one of you to learn how your path unfolds, how the changes manifest in each of your lives. Is your passage easy or hard, smooth or bumpy? Are you experiencing things that I experienced or totally different ones that leave you in fear or confusion or awe and wonder?

No matter your experience, please pat yourself on the back and give yourself credit for having had the courage to consciously awaken. Congratulate yourself for being a pioneer and leading the way for the millions who will follow and finally, give yourself some time to adapt, adjust, and assimilate all you have learned and experienced.

The changes we humans are going through are not small or insignificant. They require time to be understood and practiced. They reflect a world in upheaval. They may be absorbed in a nano-second or be understood slowly and gradually over time. Whatever is your path, it is the right one for you. Whatever is your understanding is the right understanding. The book you hold in your hands shares my experience and my understanding.

Your experience and your comprehension are equally valid and important. Together... we, you and I, are all creating the world in which we, our children and our grandchildren will be living in the future.

What is exciting and I believe, important, is that we open our eyes, take off our blinders and see what we have never seen before. We are brave to do that. You are brave to do that.

Those who follow us will continue the evolutionary process we experience today.

IT WILL BE WONDROUS TO SEE WHAT UNFOLDS...

GLOSSARY OF DEFINITIONS—

An Energetic Perspective

Activation — The process of making someone or something fully operative, or in energetic terms, catalyzing humans into greater consciousness and awareness of the Universe and their role in it.

Allergies/congestion — In the physical world, an allergy is a physical response to a physical allergen or irritant. In the energetic realms, what appears to be a physical condition is actually an *energetic* reaction to overload.

Anchor — An energetic worker who provides stability in an unbalanced situation.

Angelic realm — The energetic state beyond the veil in which angels are said to reside.

Angels — The three-dimensional label for other-dimensional beings who are believed to act as attendants or messengers of God.

Archangels — A very specific group of angels of very high rank and having special powers.

Artifacts — Traditionally, artifacts are man-made objects of cultural or historic interest, such as an archaeological urn. In energetic terms, artifacts are the objects of a given consensus reality that define and substantiate that reality. Tables and chairs, for example, are the physical artifacts of a reality that is actually energetic.

Ascension — From a three-dimensional perspective, ascension refers to spiritual evolution. From an *energetic perspective*, it refers to the movement from physicality to an energetic state and from individuality to becoming part of the collective.

Attraction — The force under whose influence objects tend to move toward one another. It's the process whereby one thing or person aligns with another or acts like a magnet to another.

Auric field — The emanation of energies surrounding a person, place or thing, viewed by some as the essence of that individual or place, discernible by people with special sensibilities and in photos taken with special cameras equipped to perceive and record high frequencies, invisible to the rest of us.

Axis mundi — An energetic concept and location where the seemingly horizontal axis of space meets and crosses the seemingly vertical axis of time.

'Being out on a limb' — A phrase made popular by Shirley Maclaine in her book, *Out on a Limb,* to signify taking a huge risk of a leap of faith.

Bellows — A device used to blow air on and activate a fire. *Energetically,* it refers to someone who activates and enlivens a field, person or situation.

Beyond the veil — The energetic location that is separated from and different than the physical third dimension.

Bi-location — The ability to physically appear or function in two locations simultaneously.

Bio-diversity — The variety of species that naturally co-exist in a habitat or ecosystem. Only humans farm one species of vegetation at a time, thereby countering the natural laws of growth and sustainability.

Bio-diversity credits — The sale on the stock exchange of credits for carbon usage. Unlike the original carbon credits, these bio-diverse credits will be issued only for the support of a rich variety of plant material. Monocultures would no longer qualify.

Bio-recycling — The process whereby seeming waste is transformed into a valuable resource. For example, the ReGenesis Soil Company transformed organic food waste from restaurants and green grocers into laboratory tested, biologically rich humus.

Bleed-through — The experience of being in more than one-dimensional reality simultaneously.

Blended state — The energetic state that combines and contains characteristics of both the physical and energetic realities. While retaining a physical body, a being in this state exhibits characteristics of both realms, is able to function in either, but is focused on and lives primarily in a blend of the two. In this reality, a being is able to utilize a wider range of energetic frequencies than are available in the third dimension or the bridge state. The blended state is the state into which one moves on the evolutionary path after the bridge state.

Breath of Fire — A special pattern of rapid breathing, similar to panting, used in the Kundalini Yoga practice.

Bridge state — The energetic state that connects and offers passage between the three-dimensional physical world and the energetic non-physical fourth dimensional state beyond the veil. *In this state an energy worker can simultaneously be the creator of the bridge, a participant on the bridge and act as the bridge itself.* The bridge state is the first state on the evolutionary path of consciousness out of physicality.

Carbon credits — An exchange system whereby the carbon footprint of a person or business is offset by the planting of trees, the purchase of solar panels, the generation of wind energy, *or the payment of an equivalent amount of funds to be used for the creation of alternative energy.*

Catalyst — A person or thing that precipitates a physical, chemical or energetic change.

Catchment — The area into which rain, lake, and river water naturally flows.

Cellular response — When the cells of one's body seem to speak to that being, either in an ache or pain or in an activation of some sort—unseen, but subtly felt.

Change agent — In energetics, a change agent refers to a being who activates transformation without necessarily undergoing the change herself.

Channel — A physical being who is able to act as a conduit for the energy of, the information from, or the voice of an out-of-body being.

Co-fusion — Where one state or condition backs up into and interferes with another state or condition.

Collective consciousness — The pattern of thought consciously agreed on by the mass of humanity, for example, to obey traffic signals.

Collective unconscious — An unaware, agreed upon belief pattern. We are not aware of our ability to manifest through our thoughts.

Conglomerate beings — Beings that are not single entities or souls, but are rather created out of different and specific aspects of several entities. When this occurs, it's for a specific purpose from the meta-perspective.

Conjured up beings — Beings that appear to be magically created, for they have not come through the birth canal. In reality, they are energetically manifested through means unfamiliar and unacknowledged by the consensus reality of the third dimension.

Consciousness — *Awareness* by the mind of itself, of the world, and of the reality beyond the five senses.

Consensus reality — The beliefs about the world, often unconscious, agreed upon by the mass of humanity. In this perception, the objects and artifacts of the three-dimensional world are said to be solid and physical. The beliefs of the consensus reality emerge from many varied beliefs as they are reflected back and forth from the people to the grid through the "light workers" until concurrence is reached.

Containment — The action of keeping a substance or energy under control or within limits. It speaks not only of the control of a toxic poison or a spreading disease, but also of the control of an energy that is out of balance with the rest of the field, with other fields around it, or with a highly balanced field. Manifestation and transformation are optimized when clear, balanced frequencies are present.

Cross-overs — Energetic beings who cross over the bridge between dimensions and physicalize into human form. These beings are here to aid the planet and humankind as it evolves.

Damper — A metaphoric description of an energy worker who is acting to subdue, reduce or inhibit the occurring conditions.

Dimensional divide — The veil or the energetic, non-physical barrier that separates life in the third dimension from life in the other dimensions.

Dimensions — Dimensions are different states of energetic reality each of which is defined by its frequency rate. The third dimension, encompassing the first and second dimensions, has a relatively slow frequency. Across the veil, the frequencies of the fourth and the other dimensions become gradually more rapid until physicality and time are no longer present.

Ecology — Traditionally, ecology has been the study of the relationship between one organism and another, and their environment. Energetically, ecology refers to the relationship between the other dimensional energies and the denser energies of the material world.

Ecology of the cosmos — A way to describe energetics *or* the study of all energy, encompassing the outer reaches of space and the inner depths of our minds.

8.8.8/ August 8, 2008 — The date around which a very powerful inflow of energy from the higher dimensions occurred and initiated major shifts in the general consciousness of the planet.

Energetic sustainability — Sustainability has traditionally referred to the physical survival of a species, the depletion of natural resources, and the preservation and maintenance of balance. In this book, I am expanding the meaning to encompass all that accompanies, surrounds and infuses the physical reality, for example, humanity needs more than water to survive; it needs to understand the messages from the unseen world conveyed by that water.

Energetic throughway — The quasi-physical connection or energetic bridge between the third and other-dimensional realms, along which information flows between dimensions, and manifestation occurs. It's created and maintained through telepathic communication and resonance between beings on both sides of the veil.

Energetics — The study, work and focus on the vibrations that make up all life.

Energetic wormhole — A configuration of frequencies that coalesce to form a quasi-physical state.

Energy beings — A conglomeration of moving molecules that takes the form of a human being or a being with less physicality from across the veil.

Energy workers — Those who focus on and work with the myriad of frequencies that originate beyond the veil.

Etheric plane — The level of consciousness loosely connected to the third dimension but not as dense or physical.

Evolution — The process by which living organisms develop.

Evolutionary path — From the energetic perspective the evolutionary path of humankind is transformation from dense physical presence and limited consciousness to a more awakened, expanded consciousness, in a gradually less and less dense physical body.

Extra-terrestrials — Beings who reside primarily in the energetic realms beyond, not in, or on this planet. There are, however, extra-terrestrials who cross the dimensional divide and reside on earth and on other planets in many different forms.

Field — The energy of or surrounding a dynamic and constantly changing area of time and space, potentially encompassing the physical, geological, social, emotional, political, and other-dimensional qualities, individually, collectively and/or simultaneously.

Focused attention — When the focus of one's energy is like a laser beam blocking out all extraneous inputs.

Fourth dimension — *In this book* the fourth dimension refers to *all* dimensions beyond the physical. However, the guides have indicated that the fourth dimension is also a primarily energetic, and *quasi-physical* location in which a shadow of physicality is present.

Fourth sector — The area of enterprise traditionally found in the philanthropic sector, now established as for-profit ventures, in which goals are more humanitarian, just and ecological than commercially based enterprises.

Frequency — A particular vibration occurring or being repeated over and over again in a particular period of time at a set rate. *The more frequencies a person has, the greater is his/her ability to process and interpret the Universe.*

Funnel — *Physically*, a device, wide at the top and narrow at the bottom, used to guide liquid or powder into a small opening. *Metaphorically*, it refers to an energy worker who receives intense and expansive other-dimensional energies, passes them through his/her body or instrument, *transducing* or transforming them so that the population at large can receive the vibrations.

Frequency — The rate at which a vibration occurs as in sound, radio or light waves. A frequency refers to a particular energetic symbolic signature.

Grid — An energetic configuration around the earth composed of many varied thought forms or frequencies. It reflects back to earth the thoughts of the *consensus reality*. Light workers work energetically to hold the grid in place.

Grow-Operative — A cooperative program designed at the ReGenesis Farm to enable farmers to lease agricultural land and facilitate their interaction to maximize their operations and their profit.

Guides (the non-physical type) — Other-dimensional beings from beyond the third dimension who offer their direction, wisdom and assistance to humankind to enable the physically safest, energetically most appropriate and most evolved outcomes possible.

Guidance — Wisdom or input from a source beyond the veil or beyond the third dimension.

Gut level response — A response based on intuitive knowing. Such a response is not substantive or provable. It's a way of knowing based on the energy present, and offering a kind of bleed-through from the fourth dimension to the third dimension that enables the three-dimensional individual to just *know* and *accept* that knowing.

Hay bale system of growing — Physically, it's the method of growing herbs and/or vegetables in a dense layer of live compost on top of hay bales. Energetically, it refers to the layering of one frequency on another thereby enriching the cultivation process and the resulting produce.

Higher dimensions — All dimensions beyond the third and beyond the veil that contains limited form or time.

Higher energies — Higher energies are those vibrations or accelerated frequencies that exist in the realms beyond the three-dimensional world.

Higher self — That aspect of one's being that is connected to Source, that knows *truth*.

Homeopathy — A non-allopathic, healing modality in which minute diluted doses of substances that would normally cause an imbalance are used to cure that same imbalance.

Inspiration — Knowledge from an unknown three-dimensional source that one never had before without a rational explanation.

Intuition — Understanding or having knowledge without conscious reasoning. This information can be sourced in the third dimension or from the other dimensions.

Is-ness — A state of being without polarity or relativity; it exists.

Janie Appleseed — The female version of the American hero who planted apple trees across the western United States. As Johnny Appleseed scattered physical seeds, the author, Elaine Seiler, a Janie Appleseed, plants energetic seeds.

Karma — The result of an individual's actions in this and past lives which provides the guidelines for a soul's evolutionary journey. It's based on cosmic justice or what has been earned or caused in those lifetimes.

Kleinian psychoanalysis — A specific form of psychoanalysis, developed by Melanie Klein, a contemporary of Freud. This therapeutic process is based on the theory known as "object relations", which speaks to the mind's ability to distinguish between objects external to itself and the internalized images of those same objects.

Laws of the Universe — The regulations that govern how life functions in the three-dimensional world in this Universe. Other laws may guide other Universes. These laws are not created by man, but are the rules that regulate the essential physics of our world.

Light being — A non-physical being composed of the frequency of light.

Light workers — A sub-set of energy workers who work with the frequencies of light doing many varied specific tasks, each of which require very specific energetic frequencies like grid workers, Reiki practitioners and medical intuitives.

Lightning rod — *Physically* a metal rod fixed to a building to divert lightning harmlessly into the ground. *Energetically*, it refers to a person or thing that attracts energetic attention in order to accomplish a goal.

Living laboratory — A contained and structured environment in which a focus, premise or concept is tested.

Living systems — An interconnected network modeled after a natural organism or process.

Magical thinking — Thoughts based on the belief that if one thinks something is so, it will be so.

Magnetize — To align the frequencies between objects or persons in such a way as to create an attraction between them.

Merkabah — Traditionally Merkabah referred to the chariot of Ezekiel in the Bible. In sacred geometry it refers to the energetic configuration of two intersecting tetrahedrons and is used in meditation.

Metaphor — A person, place, animal or thought that stands for or acts as a symbol of something else. For example, the unseasonable and excessive rain experienced in Australia is a metaphor for the cleansing force of nature.

Morphogenetic field — All the energies contained within a given space and time area.

Multidimensional — *(without a hyphen)* A human being who lives in many different realms in this three-dimensional world. A person who is a hippie in his free time and a suited lawyer in his professional life, is an example of a multidimensional being.

Multi-dimensional — *(with a hyphen)* A human being who is connected to and lives on many different dimensions or energetic realms.

Multi-dimensional partnering — Sharing, caring, helpful, cooperative energy between two or more individuals from different dimensions, focused on a mutual goal.

Multi-dimensional transformation — Change that takes place in the physical world when energies from beyond the veil, or from the other dimensions are introduced. The change is qualitatively different than change made with three-dimensional input.

Netti pot — A small pitcher-like pot used for nasal irrigation.

Negative thought — A thinking process generally characterized by a focus on non-positive outcomes such as illness, or crisis.

Numerology — The study of the meaning and symbolic interpretation of numbers.

On-line — A phrase used to describe energy or light workers at work.

Off-line — A phrase used to describe the inactive state of energy workers.

Organic farming — Farming naturally, without the use of chemical fertilizers, hormones, weed preparations, or genetically modified seeds.

Organic weed control systems — Non-chemical organic combinations used to control weeds and plant imbalance.

Other realms — States of being and consciousness beyond the physical world.

Out-of-body beings — Beings with no corporal reality from beyond the physical realm.

Overshadow — A soul or energetic being capable of sharing its energetic essence with a physical being.

Parallel realities — A variety of states of being that exist simultaneously, superimposed or adjacent to each other.

Partnering energy — A quality of energetic sharing that may or may not be intimate focused on a particular goal without time or space limitations.

Past lives — Prior lifetimes.

Pendulum — A divination tool using the body's electrical energy, to reveal a yes or no answer to a question. A pendulum is any weighted object hanging from a cord, chain or necklace, essentially anything that can swing freely. It is held in one's hand in such a way as to become a physical extension of one's body's energy or electric system.

Permaculture — The system of agricultural cultivation developed by Bill Mollison that is reflective of natural systems and intended to be sustainable and self-sufficient.

Phase shift — A transition between various energetic states during which a being's energy is reconfigured.

Planes — States of reality that have geographic or geometric homogeneity in the third dimension and energetic homogeneity in the other realms.

Prayer — A *three-dimensional request* for assistance, input, or intercession from the other-dimensional realms. Prayer becomes *other-dimensional* when the experience is mystical and *transformative*.

Quantum physics — The branch of science concerned with the nature and properties of matter and energy at an extremely minute level.

Reality — A lived experience that does not require a reference to any location, time or space.

Realm — Either a three-dimensional place, bound by time and space, or a multi-dimensional state without those limitations.

Reciprocity — The process by which one space or person is energetically linked to and from one another.

Reflection — The process in which a space or person mirrors something from another space or person.

Regeneration — The trimming and weeding of remnants of rainforest trees to allow and encourage the natural re-seeding and growth of the original species.

Regeneration plantings — The planting of original rainforest trees to facilitate growth where it was once abundant.

ReGenesis Farm — An organic farm initiated by Elaine Seiler outside Byron Bay, Australia in 2001 and referred to in this book as a vehicle through which she learned about energetics.

Religion — A three-dimensional concept referring to the worship of a specific deity or deities in a specific way, prescribed by the tenets of that school of thought.

Resonance — Traditionally used in science to describe the prolongation of a vibration by oscillating it back and forth from one surface to another. In *energetic* terms, it refers to the state or process whereby two or more disparate frequencies are harmonized or synchronized until balance is achieved.

Resonant energies — Those with harmonious vibrations.

Resonator — A person able to express frequencies in such a way as to create a reverberation in the field and to do this over and over again, until balance is achieved.

Saints — Individuals who, after death, are acknowledged by the Christian Church as being of extreme virtue. They are venerated and the object of prayers for intercession.

Selenium — A mineral considered valuable to boost the immune system.

Sensitive — A person who is able to link his/her energies to beings in the other dimensions and translate or bring through information from those realms.

Shadow — Energetically, a shadow refers to the toxic residue of an individual or group's negative thoughts.

Shaman — A person predominantly from an indigenous culture, having access to the spirit world, primarily through ritual, divination or trance.

Shift fallout — The by-product of a change in an energy field.

Soul — The immaterial aspect of a human or animal that is thought to exist independent of its physical expression and to continue indefinitely.

Soul groups — A collective of beings whose frequencies are similar and whose souls are energetically connected.

Soul partner — A being whose energy is so harmonious, resonant and aligned with another's that together they form a unique resonant relationship, usually one of a kind and lasting over several lifetimes.

Soul's work — The gifts, lessons, challenges, and commitment of a being coming into a physical body.

Space continuum — A continuous sequence of locations or frequencies lined up one next to another in which adjacent elements are not perceptibly different, but as one progresses along the lineup, it becomes apparent that the extremes at each end are distinct.

Spirit — From a traditional perspective, Spirit refers to God. From an energetic perspective, Spirit indicates the joining of consciousness of all energetic beings.

Spirituality — A three-dimensional belief in a power or powers beyond this realm. Unlike religion, there are no proscribed forms or format for its expression.

Stewardship — Responsibility for, as well as responsiveness to, the earth and all her creatures.

Substantiation — The process whereby an energy being takes on material form. This requires that the new being has within her the full range of frequencies required for physical life on earth.

Sustainability — Traditionally, sustainability has meant lasting into the future by avoiding the depletion of natural resources. From an energetic viewpoint, balance is essential. The energies *resulting from* the efforts of each project must be equal or greater than the energies *put into* it.

Symbolic message — An interpretation gained through a metaphor.

Synchronicity — "The simultaneous occurrence of events that appear related but have no discernible causal connection." (Oxford Dictionary) These seeming coincidences form the energetic bridge between the material and subtle realms.

Swales — Low or hollow depressions in the earth, created to enable drainage between planting rows in the growing system called permaculture.

Telepathy — An evolved state of consciousness that may, but doesn't necessarily include another person in which there is simply *knowing*, without research, without discussion, without rhyme or reason. This energetic state defies physicality; in it, manifestation is only a thought away.

Temporal shift — A change in time.

Third dimension — The arena of life that has physicality, where time, space, and polarities exist, where *consensus reality* has created the illusion of physicality and sentient beings react and respond to what is seemingly real through the five senses.

Time — Exists strictly in the third dimension. In the other dimensions, there is only is-ness.

A time continuum — The marking of time.

Toxicity — An imbalanced bodily state caused by a variety of substances that are unhealthy for a particular person. Toxic substances can range from true chemical poisons, like arsenic and mercury, to energies that are not balanced or in alignment with a given individual's unique state of vibrational balance.

Transducer — *Physically* a transducer is a device that transforms a frequency from one form to another, as in the AC to DC current in electricity or a loudspeaker that transforms electrical signals into sound energy. *Energetically* a transducer is a device or a person who is able to transform a very strong, powerful, and possibly damaging other-dimensional energy into a modulated frequency that can be utilized by humanity on earth.

Transformation — A thorough change in form or appearance of a person, place or thing, resulting in a totally different but equivalent expression of the original underlying vibrations or energetic make-up.

Transformation Energetics™ — The specific form of energy work done by Elaine Seiler. Multi-dimensional energies are passed through her body to clear and create balance as well as catalyze evolutionary changes in people and the planet.

Transpersonal psychoanalysis — Traditional psychoanalysis deals with emotional balance and wellbeing. Transpersonal psychoanalysis, by contrast, is the therapeutic process concerned with the recognition, acceptance and realization of ultimate states of consciousness in physical reality, as compared with states of consciousness in other dimensions like illumination, transcendence and cosmic unity.

Triple bottom line — Economic, ecological and ethical sustainability or balance.

A tuck in the road — A reduction of the time it takes to travel a distance on a physical road through intention and thought.

Tuned — Adjusted to the required or appropriate vibration.

Tuning fork — In music, a two-pronged steel device used by musicians, which vibrates when struck to produce a note of specific pitch. In *energetics*, it refers to any being or device that vibrates at a certain frequency in order to create and hold a specific resonant vibratory pattern.

Unseen realms — The invisible, non-physical realms beyond the third dimension.

Veil — The invisible divider between the physical, material world and the totally invisible, energetic other-dimensional world.

Vibrations — The oscillations of a field that give it its character, quality or atmosphere—fast, slow, cohesive, balanced, harmonious, or chaotic.

Walk-in — An energetic being, who, as part of a soul agreement, changes places with the soul of a physical being. The soul that was in the body leaves, usually after a serious accident or illness, and the new soul *walks into* and takes over that physical body at its current physical age. The new soul inherits full or partial memory of the former soul. This mutual